Letters Missionaries NEVER Write

Frederick L. Kosin

ECS
MINISTRIES
The Word to the World

Letters Missionaries Never Write

Frederick L. Kosin

Published by:
ECS Ministries
PO Box 1028
Dubuque, IA 52004-1028
phone: (563) 585-2070
email: ecsorders@ecsministries.org
website: www.ecsministries.org

First Edition 2010

ISBN 978-1-59387-117-8

Frederick and Jenny Kosin
PO Box 7505
Florence, SC 29502
Web: www.FrednJenny.com

Printed in the United States of America

Table of Contents

Introduction 5
Foreward 9
Dedication 11
1. A Missionary Candidate 13
2. A Missionary on Deputation 19
3. A Short Term Missionary 23
4. A New Missionary 27
5. A Veteran Missionary 33
6. A Missionary Kid "MK" 39
7. A Missionary on Furlough 47
8. A Missionary Mother 55
9. "Shipwrecked" Missionaries 63
10. A Retired Missionary 75
11. A Failed Missionary 79
12. A Missionary Widow 85
13. A Prepared Missionary 93
14. You Could Have Helped! 105
15. Pray For Us 117
16. Prayer Requests 131
17. Post Script 141

Introduction

This book is a collection of letters that missionaries do not write. I did not find these letters on their desks or in their computers as we traveled visiting missionaries. I don't think you will find them in print elsewhere. One of the reasons they are not in print [till now] is missionaries are not expected to write these kinds of letters. As Christians, we expect them to write about thrilling opportunities, amazing conversions, enormous changes, remarkable opposition, wonderful victories, and unusual provision—and leave unsaid their own feelings and a flat appraisal of how things are really going.

Some of these letters are long because missionaries' hearts are so full of what the Lord has given them to do. Many folk back home think missionaries have nothing else to do but write letters. It is in fact a very big item on their agenda of responsibilities. Some love to write, others loathe the job. But it is our approach to letters that force missionaries to write such short letters. "If I write a long letter they will not read it." they say to themselves or are told by others. So we are given a very small sample of what is going on. We are largely to blame for the content of their letters. Because these are letters they do not write, they are long, involved, informative and brazenly honest. When we are used to freeze dried everything we think missionary information should be equally instant and palatable.

A page entitled "A New Missionary" has been in my file for years with the word "anonymous" at the bottom. Someone gave it to me long ago and I kept it. Nothing written is truly anonymous! Every author has a name. They may wish not to reveal it, hence "name withheld." Or in manifold copying the name was dropped purposely or inadvertently and so "author unknown." Whoever the author is may I ask his/her indulgence. If you find your piece [chapter 4] drawn and quartered, I have only done so to add a dash of color from my own life and experience. Your seed has germinated and has borne many manner of fruit for the information of the Lord's people.

Apologies offered.

Caution: Dangerous medicine!

One of the greatest temptations in reading these letters is to try to figure out who wrote it, what country it was and when the situation took place. May I save a lot of trouble for yourself and your missionaries. No story is complete in any letter. Each is a fictitious composite. A kind of kaleidoscope of many experiences that we have seen, gone through or others have shared with us. Names have been left out of most of them and countries have also been deleted to insulate you from seeking to know any real missionary reflected in a letter. What you concoct in your head will only lower your estimate of any missionary and sadly misrepresent their service to the Lord. That is precisely why missionaries do not write letters like this. Because of our reaction!

It is this last item that goes on in their mind, which is often left unsaid, that provokes these "Letters Missionaries Never Write." Were we to receive them, sent to us by a known missionary, most of us would find it difficult to deal with the broken image we have proudly held up for so long. One person said they felt missionaries were "giants." But the definition of giant often includes "superhuman." That is a picture of someone without defeat or failure. Many missionaries are afraid to write of failure or give a report of a spiritual because "we could not handle it" and they are not sure what would happen.

Above all, they fear coming home as failures. The psychological experiences of "failed missionaries" is not so much their fault as the response many of us would give if we were forced to address their "default." Maybe the enclosed letters will help us face missionaries as real people who have the same feelings and problems but are often on a very high pedestal from which a fall is so much more damaging to themselves, as well as to us as spectators.

It is not my intention to "put down" missionaries or to undermine them or their ministry. We have committed ourselves to minister to missionaries, not undermine their work. We have visited missionaries in scores of countries and have observed many of the "feelings" expressed in these letters. Obviously we have not included names or countries because the conditions are not limited to any country or area of the world. The personal conditions are found in many people. But what may be surprising is that they are found in "missionaries." If we sense these feelings in people we fellowship with on a weekly basis in church we do not think much of it. But we expect missionaries to insulate us from these kinds of feelings about themselves. Missionaries are great people and have in fact left behind a multitude of things, given up an enormous amount and sacrificed far more than most of us are even willing to consider. Yet they are very normal people. It is this aspect of life that I want to convey by these letters. For many missionaries it is a very lonely isolated existence in some remote outpost in a very foreign country. Many missionaries are not at all prepared for the isolation they experience in this ministry.

I have asked many missionaries to read these letters and they thanked me for sharing this perspective on their life and ministry. They have said "I could never write that!" or "Print it! It is true." "You are right on target!" Some have made helpful comments that pinpoint the problem more appropriately. I wrote these letters to draw us closer to those who serve the Lord in foreign lands. And, yes, so you can write to them to encourage them in their service for the Lord and to the Lord. You also may be able to honestly say "I understand!"

One of their [our] greatest needs is to "pray for one another." But if we do not know the needs how can we pray intelligently for anyone, particularly someone half a world away, immersed in a totally different culture, and facing incredible opposition. At the same time we spend our efforts trying to get rich, hoping to escape problems, insulating ourselves from difficulties and generally praying nothing unusual will happen in our lives. For missionaries our prayers may be the same as for ourselves but that is not always consistent with biblical prayer.

Make sure you read Chapter 16—it contains prayer ideas stimulated by each of the letters. Pray for our missionaries!

The mission situation around the world is changing rapidly. As our world continues to alter its course as well as the speed with which it changes, the missionary community must change as well. Many missionaries find this hard to do. We ourselves find it hard to do in our church, our family and friendships in an ever evolving world. Some missionaries do not want to change anything. Others come with an agenda of change. This can and does bring clashes. These disagreements are some of the reasons we are finding the job of world evangelism so hard in a world that has the technological expertise to get the job done rapidly. But the Lord commissioned people not machines and technology to bring the good news. These letters are primarily about people. People who face problems. People who face problems while,

Serving the greatest Master.

Frederick L. Kosin

PS: Read the letters and do what Paul asks in 1 Thessalonians 5:11 "Pray for us!"

Foreward

"I have known Fred and Jenny Kosin for many years and I know they walk with God in grace and reality. This book demonstrates their great passion for God and His work across the world.

We urgently need more people with this kind of ministry. My prayer is that these pages may help people to get more involved with missionaries and God's great global program.

Please don't worry about some point in the book you don't understand or agree with, but allow the Holy Spirit to really speak to your heart even as He led the church and Paul and Barnabas in Acts 13."

–George Verwer

Dedication

Dedicated to all missionaries who are truly honest.

They have an exceptional pedigree.

Chapter 1

A Missionary Candidate

Dear Friends,

I have just finished my advanced degree in missiology. What a thrilling experience it was to study missions for three years. It is hard to imagine all that I have learned about missions and missionaries. The vast wealth of knowledge that I have been exposed to has just given me such a perspective on missions and the need to reach our world with the gospel. I never dreamed of all I would absorb from the scholarly professors of missions. I am just so thankful!

I guess that I learned more about the peoples of the world from these studies than anything else. Our study of cross cultural evangelism just made me want to go out right away to some obscure 10-40 country and just begin sharing my life and watch the principles of missions just blossom. The case studies of missionary problems were so fundamental to the overall job of missions that it seems transparent what the solutions are. It will be fun helping work out the difficulties that face so many mission strategies.

We also met so many missionaries from so many parts of the world. Some of the most fantastic people I met are missionaries. They have such a grip on the needs of the world and challenged us to be pro-active in so many areas. I just want to impact our world in such a positive way.

Since getting along with other missionaries is apparently the biggest problem on the field, my studies in interpersonal relationships will really come in handy. It will be just so useful to have analyzed all the different personality traits and be able to show how they need to be considered before assigning various people to work together. It is such a bad testimony to the world when the missionary community can't work together in harmony.

My psychology classes were so helpful. I can see counseling will be a large part of my contribution to missions. I am sure many of these problems could be avoided if we just implemented some of the recommendations of studies done in the business sector for personnel management. The application of sociological interpretation to the problems of the missionary community will enhance their usefulness and extend each individual effort and thereby shorten the time of accomplishing the Great Commission. Amen!

In our study of the gospel we learned so much about which presentation is most palatable in various cultures. It is instructive how the message can be adapted to different people groups so that the rate of refusal is down-sized considerably. The many evidences that surfaced in studies of past evangelistic pushes demonstrated the reasons people refused the gospel. Much like selling a product at home, the packaging is often more important than the content. In order to make the message attractive and acceptable to various ethnic and religious groups the wording and method of presentation is all important. I am looking forward to demonstrating how the success of missions can be significantly increased by giving attention to these simple guidelines. If I can just help in this area it will be a real contribution to world missions.

In our course on communication with the Christian sector I was greatly helped by the insights of the teachers on how to deliver a compelling message and the best ways to raise support through "prayer letters." I never realized before that strategic methods of developing partners in your service as a missionary were so consequential. I am sure that if more missionaries were to ameliorate these characteristics in their presentations, video messages, overheads and reports of the work and their missionary challenge messages we would see a greater inflow of funds. So much more could be done for the poor people of the third world if we just used more effective methods of bringing the needs to those who provide alimentation for missions. I can see that money will not be a problem since writing captivating letters with a compelling description of financial needs is quintessential to raising funds. The money is there and people just want to know where to give. Money should not hinder the service rendered by a missionary.

Goal setting has revolutionized my life. I came to university just so disorganized and felt like such a failure when we analyzed our behavioral patterns in relation to the effective use of our time and abilities in that initial review. I just cannot thank the staff enough for making me realize that I can just get so much more done in a shorter period of time by just setting attainable goals and being pro-active toward accomplishing those goals. As I set out for the mission field it has become clear that one of the reasons for our ineffectiveness is an unwillingness to accomplish specific things each day, each week and of course each term on the field. It seems so many missionaries look back and cannot define any specific accomplishments over a particular period of time. I am sure I can help streamline many of the ministries by assisting them in establishing where we are really headed. It has helped me so much I just want to help others.

In our review of Global Strategy it was just amazing to me how many missionaries we have sent to the same people over the last 200 years. Those who have heard the gospel the most in the past are hearing it the most today. It's just not fair to send missionaries to those who have repeatedly been exposed to the message when many people groups have never had an adequate presentation of the gospel. We want everyone to hear of Jesus just as soon as possible and thereby vivificate the coming of Christ. It is clear we have all the necessary tools in our day technologically to give the message to every one in our generation. We must let nothing obstruct us.

Of course one of the greatest hindrances to the spread of the gospel is the multiplicity of Christian organizations who are virtually duplicating the same assignment around the world. Such redundancy is a waste of money and manpower. There just needs to be a renewed effort to work together with all mission agencies and not be so concerned with the differences that divide us in methodology or message. Our study of religions pointed out how close we really are and showed how it is possible to harmonize if we concentrate on what unites us instead of what divides us. I hope that I can just be a peacemaker among the many mission organizations for the kingdom of God.

The course on power evangelism was fantastic. How could a person going to the mission field not consider the amazing implications of this unbelievable tool for reaching our world with the gospel in our generation. I am really looking forward to just letting the Lord do mighty works like He did with the apostles in the Book of Acts. I can hardly contain my enthusiasm. Amen!

One of the most interesting, and I must say controversial subjects in school was "Change on the Mission Field." I never realized how different the methods are between those who have been on the field forty years and those who are going out now. It was also instructive to learn how far we have come in mission effectiveness since Paul first began. Our study of Acts transformed my concept of missions and exposed the many pitfalls the early church fell into. I just can't imagine how any missionary could continue to use the colonialistic methods of missions in a day when nationalism is so strong. Surely the best part of sagacity is to use ministries and methods that have been proven in the missionary classroom over the past few years. We are living in a very different age with different problems, and different solutions. If we do not insist on change we will continue to accomplish almost nothing for the Kingdom of God.

A brief study on "How to Choose Your Mission Board" proved insightful as I head toward my final hurdles of getting to the mission field. I can see that a vocation, or profession is so important to entering some of the countries that need evangelizing the most. Just being a missionary doesn't seem to fulfill the requirements of serving the Lord any more. We live in such a sophisticated world and the demands on missionaries are so intense that it just requires higher education and a marketable skill before ever considering missions. I thank the Lord for my training.

The course on computers and the enormous resources available on the internet and the world wide web expanded my horizons beyond belief. What tools are just a click away? We can solve many problems in cross cultural ministries by the click of a button. I just did not have the time in class to be able to tap all the information at my finger tips. Once I get to the field I am looking forward to surfing the net in search of answers to questions raised in our classes. And the price of computers has come down so far, every missionary must have one even if he only uses it for his quiet-time. I found I saved so much time in my quiet-time by using the computer. I guess that sounds funny. In addition, the instant communication with my prayer partners by Email will bring their prayers right up to the moment. Wow! What a day to be serving the Lord as a missionary!

I hope that I have been able to give you a summary of how helpful the past three years have been in preparing me to serve the Lord on the mission field. I guess you can see I am really excited about serving the Lord in missions. As soon as possible I hope to get the deputation work out of the way so I can just get on with the job God called me to when I first entered college seven years ago. It has been a long time of preparation but I really feel ready to get to the field. I can hardly wait to share the gospel with my first contact.

Sincerely,

PS: I know I need your prayers. Pray that I will be able to speak without saying "just" so many times. I am sure it interferes with my presentation of the Gospel.

* * * * * * * * * * * * *

[Typical reactions to this letter have been chiefly twofold. One is to think the person is very legitimate and has a good handle on all the problems and we should encourage him/her to get to the field as soon as possible.

The other is to assume the person is not thinking realistically and feels he/she is "God's gift to missionaries." Most missionaries would be the last ones to want this person on the field with all the answers for all the problems. Many feel this person needs to spend a fair amount of time getting his/her own maturity notched up a few levels before heading to the field. This person is full of pride and themselves as a young graduate with a degree in missiology. One of the few people we do not need on the field is a person who without even being on the field knows all the problems and solutions because they sat in the classroom for a few years.] *ed*

Chapter 2

A Missionary on Deputation

Dear Bob and Sue,

We are so excited about going to the mission field and are trying to get the necessary support so we can get to the field and begin the wonderful work that the Lord has laid on our hearts. The need of the mission field has been on our hearts for a long time and we have concluded it is the God's will for us to go. So many things have fallen into place over the past few months, how can we doubt the Lord has called us to serve Him?

But we have been presenting our call to a lot of churches and visiting many friends and still are not fully supported. Our mission board is concerned that maybe we should not go to the field after all. How can there be such a seeming contradiction between what the Lord has done for us over the many months and the board saying that because the support level is so low we should consider not going? Over this time we have gone from an emotional and spiritual high to the edge of serious discouragement and despondency. Are we to listen to the Lord who has called us or to the mission board who is telling us how much we must raise? This is just one of the many questions that dog our steps every day.

We also have some serious questions about this method of getting to the field. It seems we are not to question the board's decisions of setting a specific dollar amount we are supposed to raise before we leave for the field. Where is the idea of raising "support" found in the New Testament? We go to the Bible for our doctrine of Salvation, our guidelines for discipleship, the principles of marriage, how to raise children and how to live as Christians in the world. Why do we not go to the same book for how the Lord's work should be supported? What does Philippians 4:19 mean to those of us who want to serve the Lord on the mission field? Do the principles of missions that guided the church 175 years ago not work any more? Since the Lord supplied the needs of "faith" missionaries like George Muller, Hudson Taylor, and Fred Arnot without raising any funds or having a board set a support level, can't the Lord do the same for us today? Have we in our modern era organized the Lord and the Holy Spirit right out of His miraculous work of supplying our needs? Who can say what our needs will be from month to month and year after year on a mission field that varies with so many factors? Does raising support cause us to look to man more than to God for our needs? Is the scripture equally relevant in all areas of missions?

We are frankly very confused! I am sorry to have to write to you like this, but who can we talk to who understands us? I hope you will not think us unspiritual because of all the questions. We have prayed and don't seem to get answers. We listen to the board and they don't seem to hear us. Sometimes we just sit and cry!

It is hard in the midst of speaking to various churches and meeting with mission committees not to be bothered by many of these questions. On top of all of that, it makes me feel like a beggar sitting with a missions committee of a church I do not attend and asking them to promise to support us $50.00 or $75.00 monthly. It all seems to boil down to our ability to give a good sales pitch or present an exciting delivery of what we hope to do. Most church mission committees are trying to support more missionaries than they can afford. And we want them to add us to their list!

We haven't even been to the field and we wonder if we are going to get there. Are we unsuitable or unqualified to serve because of these questions or is there something out of balance in the system of getting into missions? The Lord has called us and we are sure that He wants us to go but we are being blocked by, well, our ability to raise funds from people who are already giving a lot to missions.

This letter is not to ask you for funds but to air out many of the questions we have about the whole system of getting to the field. We value your counsel and would appreciate it if you would let us know what your thoughts are. Should we consider changing mission boards?

Should we try to go anyway and believe the Lord has called and will supply our needs? Is it people who are unwilling to obey the Lord and give to us so we can go? Surely there are people in the churches who should give so we can go but are just unwilling to sign a faith promise. Is it the church's fault or ours that we feel the way we do? Should we consider giving up our calling and return to our secular jobs and realize that the Lord was not calling or we misread what the Lord was asking us to do? To say we are not going could seriously affect many young Christians we told about missions. We ourselves would feel like such failures if we decided we are not going after all we have said and done. As you can see we are confused and really wonder what is happening.

The Bible is so clear that the world needs to be evangelized and the prayer we are to pray is that the Lord would "send laborers into His field." We have prayed that prayer. We are ready to go. The only link in this broken chain is financial support. Are we to take that one thing as the Lord giving us the reason not to go?

Thanks for your friendship. We have found very few friends we can really talk to or personally write about our feelings. Missionaries are supposed to be sort of "super saints" without the kind of doubts we seem to be having. We do not doubt the Lord but we are finding it difficult not to doubt our missions committee, mission board, the church and Christians in general. It seems so contrary to the vast need for missions with us sitting at home not able to go because of money.

Thanks again for letting us share our heartache with you. We would love to hear from you.

In the service of the Lord,

PS: I guess I did not mention that we need your prayers. But you must know that is true now more than ever before. Thanks!

Chapter 3

A Short Term Missionary

Dear Friends,

I have just returned from one of the most exciting experiences of my life. For me a short term experience in missions was just what I needed to give me fresh insight into life and missionary service. Missions will now be a special option for me as I continue my education and plan for my future. I want to thank you for sharing in my experience and for helping my trip to be a success. I had no idea what to expect when I volunteered to go to South America for six weeks. Let me take a few minutes of your time to share what we did and what I learned.

The first week was spent in orientation and getting to know the members of my team. It was interesting to get to know so many young people from other parts of the country. We also learned from missionaries who had been on the field. There were others who gave us exciting Bible studies and showed us how to use the Bible in our daily life. One of the most interesting times was the introduction to South American culture and particularly the country we would be visiting. We felt so prepared to help missionaries who live and work there. I also got to know Becky who has become an important part of my life. She and I are both 17 years old.

I wasn't really sure what I was signing up for when I agreed to go. But a bunch of others were going so I thought it would be fun. I had never been out of the country and so I had to get some shots and a passport. The thrill of leaving our country and going to another one just gave me goose bumps. It was awesome just to think about it. My parents bought me some new clothes, and I was supposed to bring a box of tools. I bought a new Bible just for this trip. I found people who were willing to help pay my expenses for getting there and back.

One of the purposes of this trip was to get a feel for missions. Another was to give us a personal experience in missions. A third was for us to meet and get to know a real missionary. We were also sort of trying it to see if we liked it enough to do it more, maybe two years or something like that. The staff also hopes that this face to face encounter in missions will help us consider missionary work as a life vocation.

This was the fist time I ever flew an airplane. Wow! What an experience. It is really just amazing to be a missionary and travel so far so fast. There were a few of the others who got sick. What a mess the guy next to me made. The smell was terrible. He did not know what the little bags were for. He was the really macho guy at orientation but what a wimp on the plane. He said he would never be a missionary if it means flying. The meals were great and it was really fun being served by the hostesses. They were cute.

As I look back on my six weeks I can honestly say that my life will never be the same. A number of very profound things happened during this time. I shall never forget the poverty I saw when we arrived in that country. I had no idea that people lived in such unbelievable conditions. That helped me be far more thankful for my home, my room and for the job my dad has that makes it possible for me to live like we do. The food we ate was all right but the people on the street ate what I thought was garbage. I guess I really ought to be more thankful for the food mom puts in front of me. It was also a big discovery to me that missionaries live very simply. I thought missionaries who went out were so holy and such giants spiritually that they would be totally out of touch with us guys. It was really amazing to me that they got down and worked right with us in the building project. That was really so cool. They even played in some of the games in the evening. That was totally awesome.

Another thing that really impressed me was the opportunity to live with guys from several parts of the country. It was very interesting to get to know different people from various churches and have long discussions about how churches function, the leaders, the youth group activities, and what various verses in the Bible mean. I was really struck by some of the ones who came and I wondered how they got there. They seem so out of touch with life in general. One guy said he had never been to a movie in his whole life and thought that real Christians shouldn't go to movies. It made us feel funny when most of the rest of us were comparing which movies we saw and which were the best. There were also some really good looking girls on our team. It was good to know that it wasn't just the "plain Janes" interested in missions.

I found it challenging to work along with the "nationals" in the building project. It was fun to learn a few words in Spanish and try them out with the guys who were doing the building. I can see the need to send more missionaries down to help them out. At times I wondered what I could do after I got back to help in missions.

It was a surprise to me what missionaries did. I guess I really never paid attention to missionaries when they spoke at our church. I enjoyed the pictures but never checked in when they were telling what it was they did. The first hand experience helped me learn that missionaries do a lot of stuff that people do right here in our country. I found out that a lot of missionaries are doctors, nurses, teachers, farmers, and of course they all do a lot of preaching and sharing the gospel. I guess it was a surprise to me that during the orientation we were taught how to share the gospel with someone else. I don't think I have ever done that, even though I have been a Christian since I was 8 years old.

When we got home we had a big meeting to share our experiences and tell the leaders what we got out of the six weeks. I was surprised that some of the kids said they had made a commitment to be a missionary and were going to alter their whole life so they could become a missionary. Some gave some very special testimonies of how they would pray and give a lot of money to missions. That was truly awesome. A few had a bad time because the rules were so stiff they couldn't stay out late at night and couldn't spend much time with the girls. I sure would like to have seen Becky more than at meals and in church.

For me it was mainly an awakening to the many things I had to be thankful for living in America and being in a Christian home and all that stuff.

We were also asked to write a letter to everyone who had helped us do this mission trip and to all who had prayed for us. So that is why I am writing to thank you for helping me and I hope you feel that your helping me has not been in vain. I hope that I can help people better after seeing the needs in South America.

Sincerely,

PS: It was so much fun, that I am thinking of doing it again next year to a different country if Becky does. I hope you will help me again. I will write again if I end up going.

Chapter 4

A New Missionary

Dear Friends,

I am a new missionary. I felt the call to missions and was deeply convicted by the need in missions. I studied the world picture. I was compelled by the lack of missionaries, by the millions who are dying without Christ, by the many in our world who have never heard of Jesus Christ. I left my family, my job and home to fulfill the great commission.

I came out to the field a very holy and sanctified woman. I do not wear makeup or jewelry, my dresses have sleeves, I do not wear pants or shorts and my skirts cover my knees. I have my quiet time each day, but I have discovered a dirty heart within.

Since the day I arrived on the mission compound I have struggled with "missions." I have asked myself again and again "What is missionary work?" "You must not give to beggars," the senior missionaries told me. At least, "if you must, do not give more than a penny." I walked out of a market a few days later. A skinny boy with big brown eyes held out his dirty little hand. His little sister in a filthy tattered dress followed him. I glanced around. No one was watching. I put a few coins in his hand. He went away with a smile. Now every day from morning till night we have a stream of beggars at our door. The other missionaries cannot understand why so many have come so suddenly. I did not tell them I gave a boy some coins in the market. I do not dare answer the door, either; they will recognize me.

My family and friends from home send parcels of used clothing for me to give to the poor. After I began to distribute to the beggars in the village a whole line of people waited at my cottage for my used clothes. I was told not to "give" the clothes away. "Use the clothes as money to pay your gardener or your house girl." But these clothes were given to me to give away not to "sell" to the poor or pay my workers! I came to the mission field to give, not to barter and sell what had cost me nothing.

I gave up my profession, left my home and family to bring the good news to people who have never heard it. I came to love them, sit where they sit, eat what they eat, speak like they speak, to heal their diseases, play with their children, feed their bodies, put my arms around them, teach them the scriptures and give myself to them. I came to pour my life out like my Lord did for me.

A feeble woman came to our door. Her face was twisted in a pathetic appeal for us to treat her very sick little baby. She pulled back the foul rag covering the little bundle in her frail arms. I could count the ribs. I wanted to take her in and love her and show her that someone cared about that feverish baby. My senior worker said, "It's past clinic hours. You must come back tomorrow." But she did not come back tomorrow. I learned later she didn't come back because she didn't have a baby to bring. I wept in silence so my senior missionary would not know.

Each week I give my empty tin cans to the women who come to sell vegetables at my back door. Now most of the women that come to the mission compound selling vegetables come to my house first. I couldn't understand why! Before dawn there would be a dozen ladies selling vegetables at my verandah. A veteran missionary told me "You must sell your tin cans like all the other missionaries." But I can't sell tin cans to the poorest people I know on earth. How can I sell what I threw away back home? I came to give not sell.

I feel the heat and watch the perspiration running down my arms. I try to keep the sand and dirt from my desk. It is hard to read at night because the moths cluster around the light on my page. I do not mind these things. But I mind when my fellow missionaries cannot eat what I have cooked. "What is this?" they ask in disdain. They ask this because I come from North America and have not learned that missionaries from other places do not like to have hot served with cold, savory with sweet. My view of missionaries is being challenged every day!

Last week I got a small package in the mail. I was so thrilled to know someone had sent it. The senior missionary said I should not be getting packages because it costs a lot to get them here. I opened it, the candy bars were melted, the crackers and cheese had ants in them and a fragrant bar of soap made the chocolate taste funny. I laughed. I don't often laugh any more but I did. I thought how sweet and loving to send me a package. It took months to get here and the mice left some calling cards behind but it was great to get a box filled with love and care.

I wrote to one of my supporting churches a while back. They sent me $25.00 a month. In the letter I told them of my life, my ministry, my schedule, my house, my food, and the customs we are learning. I also told them I had fresh strawberries for lunch one day a few months ago. We have a patch in the front garden and they take no care and bear prolifically up here in the hills. I got a letter yesterday from that church. They are not going to support me any more. They said "if you can afford fresh strawberries in the middle of winter you don't need our support." I sat down and cried. What can I write to them? I haven't written them yet. I hurt too much.

I am now able to meet all those dedicated missionaries I have been reading about in the missionary magazines and praying for all these years. James is a very spiritual man but he likes to flirt. Mr. Thompson lost his temper with a man who repairs vehicles on the mission station last week. Miss Smith and Mrs. Anderson stood in front of the school arguing about some pencils last Friday.

Now I am ashamed to tell them of the power Christ has to change us and make us new creatures. But I do not forget the cesspool I have inside.

God has called me and that is why I am still here. He has promised to hold my hand. He does! That is why I did not go home last month. That is why I do not give myself to discouragement now. That is why I strengthen my commitment as I read of the Lord Jesus who "went about doing good" and said "It is more blessed to give than to receive."

Now I know what to pray: "Lord, teach Mr. Thompson patience with the other men, even though he has so much to do and it's hot and the sand is always blowing. Help James to realize that what he does, does not make us feel good. Also fill the heart of Miss Jones with love for the people. She has been here a long time and has become immune to the pleas of frail women with sick babies in their arms. Teach Mrs. Anderson that people are more important than things. Teach us all that what you are doing in us is more important than what we want to get done. Help us all learn that we are here to sacrifice our lives not to satisfy ourselves. We need to learn that every thing we do is a reflection of Your life in us whether it is preaching or just walking across the compound. We need to learn that we are being watched all the time. And Lord teach me to have a good sense of humor!"

Since I am a new missionary I can say that my preparation for coming to the field was so inadequate. I can remember the elders of my church just saying that everything would work out because the Lord would be with me and that I had a lot to give as a person. There are so many things that surprised me when I arrived I cannot begin to tell you all of them. Some of them I will never tell anyone. It would have been so helpful if we had input or some orientation from missionaries who had been on the field where we were going to serve. I wish some were honest enough to "tell it like it is." There are people who travel and visit missionaries and they could have helped us so much but the elders just thought everything would be all right. They seem so out of touch with the mission field and even missionaries. Some missionaries have left already because they had no idea what they were in for till they arrived. Some of the simplest things could have been told us if someone had the foresight to share those things. Even after I have been here such a short time I would tell new missionaries things I never thought of till it was too late.

I also pray, "Lord, I want to keep my eye on you, and off of the many faults I see in others. I do not want to become fainthearted and weary because the mission field is not all I expected. I want to stay faithful to the call which you have given me even though the call is much different than I expected. I want to be like you even if it means being much different from others around me."

Yes, I am a new missionary.

For the Lord's sake,

PS: I have not shared these things with you to make you despise missionaries. But I think you should know that I have discovered missionaries are real people. We need your prayers.

Chapter 5

A Veteran Missionary

Dear Partners,

We came out to the field many years ago with a dedication to the Lord and the gospel that made me leave my family, my home, my job, and the promised success and affluence of my home land. My wife and I left our parents and made the six week journey by ship, boat, dugout and on foot to arrive deep in the interior of the land to which the Lord had called us. We faced hardships on our trek that would have turned back many faint hearted. But we came to give our life, not just two years. We came to learn the language which no other missionary had done. We did not do any deputation work before we went out. We believed we had a call from God and He would supply all our needs. We did not arrange with a commercial company to mail out our prayer letter. We did not go to Bible School, missionary preparation and orientation school. We felt that the preparation of the Lord was enough. We went out like Abraham not knowing where we were going but sure the Lord called us to go.

When we left our country we brought only what we could carry in our five suitcases. We built a mud hut and cooked over an open fire. We planted a garden with a few seeds we brought with us. We learned to live with bugs, snakes and wild animals. We did all our shopping in the village learning the culture and the language as we went. We did not spend a year building a house, or months putting in a water system, or installing electricity and solar panels. Our typewriter was the most modern invention we possessed.

It was not our intention to "try it and see if it works" or "see if we liked it" in "short term missions." Our commitment to the gospel was to serve for life whatever the cost. We have seen many try it and not like it. Some have gone home because it is too hard. Others moved to another area to start a new work. It is interesting when new missionaries come out they want to learn so much but soon they know it all. They find our ways old fashioned. They say we are only reaching a few when we could reach multitudes with new methods.

Why isn't the way the apostles did it good enough for us as well? They went out and preached the gospel and lived from day to day with the Lord providing for them. They learned to do without rather than bring half of their worldly possessions with them. Didn't the Lord send them out telling them not to take so much with them but expect that a laborer is worthy of his wage? The Lord has met the needs of a generation of missionaries who have done a work of pioneering that will be unequaled till the coming of Christ.

We served in the days before CB radios, phones, faxes, email, websites, and even the regular mail was so slow we did not hear from home for months. Many of the people we came to reach had never seen a white face before. All day we were stared at as if we had some dread disease. People came to our door all times of the day and night. It seemed that the whole day was a series of interruptions. But that's why we came.

We find it hard to understand why "new missionaries" need everything they had back home. We stand in amazement when a container or two arrive with the household goods of our new "co-workers." The list of things we help unload includes all the appliances for the kitchen, a library of books, a workshop of power tools, refrigerator and freezer, washer and dryer, and enough clothes for a lifetime. They have phones, faxes, copy machines, computers, generators, solar panels, microwaves, radios, TV, VCR, and even an electric garage door opener.

Yes we came to stay a lifetime and considered a "term" on the field about 5 years. It hardly seems possible to get anything done when the new missionaries go home on furlough every two years for six months. As soon as they get back they start planning for the next time home. They seem to go back and forth to the home land like we go to the big city for special supplies. Whatever happened to the verses about "leaving everything" to follow the Lord?

What is wrong with sending their children to the boarding school like we did? They spend so much of the day home schooling their children when they could be doing missionary work.

We came to this country to serve the people. We did not want anything elaborate but tried to live close to the nationals. For the new missionary most of his time is spent just living. There is always something to repair, replace, install, and maintain with all the modern conveniences they have. They are constantly sending home for a part for the truck, tractor, motorcycle, computer, generator, etc. If they can get it in the big city they are gone for days at a time rounding up supplies. I wonder when they have time to do missionary work. Surely they put in 8 hours a day on their job at home. I sometimes think they didn't come to do missionary work but just live here.

These new missionaries that just came have been the hardest adjustment for me in 40 years. I determined to welcome them to the field and receive them in the name of the Lord. But as soon as they got here they started to change everything we had been doing. He is a graduate of some college in missions. They have taken a course in language study. They have degrees in other things. They have more possessions than I can fit in my house. They contradict what I have been teaching. They are opposed to the way I have been doing things. It is true they are from a different country and culture but I don't think that is the problem. We really did not meet until they arrived on the field but I hoped we would be able to work together. They are supposed to be of the same group as we are but they are so different.

We have been praying for a long time for the Lord to send a couple to our area to carry on the work the Lord has blessed over the past 40 years. I was hoping this family was the answer to our prayers. We had planned to go home and leave the work in good hands. But I can't leave it with these people. How could I go home realizing that almost all I had taught was being undone. All the methods I used were being thrown out. All the songs I had translated were being set aside. We are really sick.

In fact we are not even talking to each other. They are in one of the old houses on the station but they are planning to build a big new one. They seem to have plenty of money. I find myself watching them and they are probably watching us. I wonder what they are doing. I imagine they are trying to find ways of changing everything we have done. My mind is confused and my heart is heavy when I think of the work. I catch myself planning to guard this work from these people. I am sick of myself and my thinking and I know God hates what is happening. But what can I do? I can't go to them. They will not understand. What can I confess to make things right? I think they ought to come to me but they will not change. We are locked in a struggle for power and the future of the work. The scripture cries out to me about the whole mess. Each time I sit down to read I hear the Lord saying "How good and how pleasant it is for brethren to dwell together in unity."

Shall I just go home and let it all go? But these are my children in the Lord. I have brought them into the world physically and into the family of God spiritually. I have baptized them. Appointed them as elders. I have married them and buried many of their family. We have taught their children. I have taught them the Word, discipled them, supported them, built their homes, planted their garden, healed their sick, taught them to sing. They are mine. My whole life is invested in them. What to do? What we have tried to teach for 40 years our new colleagues seem to disregard. Where is the message of sacrifice and commitment? Now it seems, all you have to do is believe and be saved. Why isn't baptism important anymore? What happened to the role of women in the church? Why are the hymns from home I translated years ago no good? Why do we have to use musical instruments for the meetings?

Sometimes I feel like I haven't done anything when I listen to the new missionaries. I must confess that I am often discouraged when I compare our lives and ministries. That is why I am writing. Not so that you will condemn new missionaries or feel sorry for veteran missionaries but so that you will know we are people who have feelings and we need your prayers.

Your Servant in our soon coming Lord,

PS: I am sorry I have written all this. But thanks for listening. I don't have anyone to talk to out here. I do not know what to do!

Chapter 6

A Missionary Kid "MK"

Dear Fellow "Kids,"

I'm an MK and I know all about what that means. We have had a wonderful opportunity that most kids never have. We have gone places most kids never went. We have experienced life on a level most kids never even dream about. But now that I have finished school I think it is time to give my real feelings.

I became a missionary kid through no choice of my own. That is true for most of us MKs. My parents felt called of the Lord to leave all the comforts of home that I was really enjoying and say good-by to friends and family that I wanted to stay close to the rest of my life. I wanted a normal life in the suburbs with all the friends I had made in my first few years of school.

But my parents made a decision to leave all this and live in a country far from everything I loved. I know my parents prayed about it and asked a lot of questions, wrote a lot of letters and tried to get to know all they could about the mission field. They talked to us about it. But what could we say. To us then, it seemed like a great experience and a real exciting change that no one we knew could have hoped for. I used to lay in bed arguing with myself about the whole decision and the plan my parents were considering.

As a Christian I thought it was my duty to follow my parents and have the same kind of commitment they had. I would pray as I went to sleep that I wanted to be a good Christian and a missionary when I grow up. I would fall asleep with the pictures missionaries showed at our church dancing in my head. What an exciting future.

Other times I would cry myself to sleep fighting the decision my dad had chosen for the whole family. I imagined the long time being away from my friends and maybe never seeing my grandparents again. Would my classmates even miss me not going to school with them? I would put my pillow over my face to keep my crying from being heard by my parents. Sometimes I wished there was some way they could go and leave me with my grandparents, Papo and Nano. I even wished they heard my crying and maybe listen to me and consider my feelings. Once or twice I wished I was dead because then I would go to heaven. That was the best thing that could happen to a person. It seemed like going all the way around the world was the worst thing that could happen to me. It was a very confusing time for me and my brothers. They were not very old so they could not understand what was happening.

I was not called to the mission field. I was not committed to go to the other side of the world to tell people about Jesus. Yes, I was a Christian. I went to church and Sunday School, and evening services but I did not begin to know all that I would go through as a missionary kid.

But we went to the mission field and of course it was so exciting to fly in a plane, my first time. Every day was a new experience with so much to see and do. It was a big adjustment not being able to talk to anybody except some other missionary kids. Some of them were not very nice since we were from a different country than they were. Others did not even speak English. We played together but they played games I never heard of and I could not play. And they did not know how to play our games.

I was able to make a good friend after a while. We did a lot of things together and found so much to do. She had been there a long time so she knew all the neat places to go. But she had to spend a lot of time doing school work. She said she was "home schooled." I told her I was going to boarding school. She did not like that. She thought that going off to boarding school was really bad. "What was wrong with my parents that they sent us away for such a long time?" she would ask. I didn't know why. I just knew that was going to happen. I didn't even know what "boarding school" meant except that I was going to be with a lot of other kids in a school where you lived and slept and ate all like one big family. That sounded really exciting.

But my friend thought my parents were somehow not as good as hers because they were sending me off. I didn't like her attitude at all. My parents said not to worry because the Lord had led them to choose to have me go to boarding school. They were sure I would like it and get a good education. Besides they said "The parents of my friend didn't do much missionary work because they spent so much time "home schooling." I didn't understand that either. Now I know what they meant.

One of the hardest times of my life was leaving for boarding school. The first time I was sent off I cried for what seemed like a month. My parents and many others felt that this was best for their ministry. We would leave our mission home [never really home] and drive the 7 1/2 hours to the school. Once or twice we got to fly. This was "the beginning of term" as it was called. The term was three months long; then we would have a month back with our parents. That was the schedule for the whole year.

When we were together as a family, between terms, we would always ask mom and dad when we were going home on "furlough." I did not even know what the word meant, at first, except that I would be able to see my friends, be back with my grandparents, go to McDonald's, eat normal food and have enough water for showers any time I wanted. But they did not even want to talk about furlough. They said that as soon as they set a date to go home their effectiveness was cut considerably because every decision was shaped by furlough. That is exactly what I wanted to happen. We wanted a date so we could start counting the days, and weeks.

When we were at school we were reminded of the sacrifice our parents had made to come to the mission field. The teachers never spoke about the sacrifice we made by going some place many of us never wanted to go. They never seemed to realize that we would rather have been back home in our own country and with our own family. We were told that the Lord's work our parents were doing was much easier because we were in boarding school.

At night we would talk about it between us girls. We got the impression sometimes that we were in the way of getting "the Lord's work" done and so off to boarding school we would go. One girl overhead her parents talking about it. They said they "would be glad when boarding school starts so they could get on with the Lord's work." She said she lay in bed and cried all night. "Why was she born if she was interfering with her parents doing the Lord's work" she thought. All eight of us left our beds, even though we were not supposed to, and sat on her bed to try to cheer her up. But we all ended up crying because we wondered if all our parents felt that way.

There were some at boarding school who really liked it. They were glad to get away from their parents and have friends their own age who were not "nationals." That is the word my parents use for the people they were preaching to. Many of these kids tried to help us understand how lucky we were to be in a foreign country and be able to do all the things missionary kids did. We knew this. We did think we were lucky to be living in another country. But our emotions were flip flopping back and forth. It was constant turmoil.

One thing we could not do was call our parents on the phone. Many of the parents didn't have a phone way out in the bush anyway, so it would not be fair for some kids to call and others couldn't. We also learned that one time a kid called his parents and cried and cried over the phone because he was so home sick. He pleaded with his parents to come and get him. But they couldn't. It was a real mess. So no one could call.

We all got homesick some time. Maybe it was a letter from our parents. Some kids got letters all the time and some even got packages of goodies. A few kids didn't get any letters from anyone. They really had a hard time. But when one got homesick the rest of us tried to help and make them feel better.

We would not tell our real feelings to the teachers or the headmaster of the school. They would give us a long lecture that we had heard a zillion times. Every couple of weeks we were supposed to write letters to our parents. Sometimes a kid would write how bad he felt and then the teachers would read it and ask the kid to write a better letter. So we were not really supposed to write our real feelings, especially when we were really little.

Even though we were five hundred miles from any place the peer pressure was great, especially when the new term began. A lot of the kids who were in "well supported" families came back with all the latest clothes and sneakers. It was no different than at home. Some of us could not afford anything new. All our clothes were "hand-me-downs" which came in packages. We got some "used" clothes that were not fit to wear on the mission field but especially at boarding school. We had to wear them until they wore out or became too small. You could always tell by the new clothes, the latest jeans and shoes who had the money. Even the latest US styles made it to boarding school and caused quite a stir. Sometimes clothes were outlawed because they were too fashionable or "worldly." The kinds of clothes kids from other countries wore were really ridiculous. They got a lot of teasing and that made it hard for them to be accepted. But they said that is what they wore at home. These things kept the staff on edge. The dress code made a lot of stuff we would wear at home outlawed.

It was always good to come to the end of term and say goodbye to the school and the teachers and head home. Some of us got to fly home but many others had a long hot trip in a truck. A few lived very close and were home in a matter of hours. When we got home the whole process began again. We were ready to go home on furlough and my parents were wanting to get on with the Lord's work.

Now I am in the US and starting college. My parents came home for a few months to get me settled in college, then they headed back with my two younger brothers. They will return to boarding school and my parents to the Lord's work. I am trying to settle in here in a very new culture. Things have changed. One of the problems I am really struggling with, because I was raised on the mission field, is I don't really fit into the American culture. But I am American and do not want to fit into the culture of the country where my parents are missionaries. I do not belong either place. But I am determined to make it here in my real home country.

I have found some other MKs among the students and that has helped. They face the same amazing adjustments that I am trying to make. The same feelings are right here that we had in boarding school. It all seems like I am reliving a period of my life that I thought was way behind me. Because I was raised on the mission field I was not up on things that are important to guys here at college. I do not have the money to buy the kind of clothes most others have. I never played sports or games so I am totally out of it so much of the time.

There are MKs who have arrived here at college and have just jumped off the deep end. This is the first time they have been free of either their parents or the boarding school. One of the kids that really flew off was a kid that was home schooled on the mission field. She did not know how to handle money, time, freedom, relations with guys, or the temptations to do things she did not even know existed. I feel sorry for her but she doesn't want me in her life.

This girl spent so little time each day in "home schooling" she thought college was going to be a party. She has already dropped a couple of courses because she is so far behind. She is really hot and heavy with a guy and unless she really changes she will be in big trouble. Her parents do not know because she can write really sweet letters. I feel so sorry for her. She was so sheltered from everything.

I know I was sheltered too, but at least there were several hundred in our school and we had some "bad" things happen like the time a couple of guys came to the girls' dorm in the middle of the night and played a tape of music real loud. We laughed at that as the staff tried to tell us how serious it was. On another occasion the guys went to the girls dorm and took the panties out of the girl's drawers. It was so funny to see them all hanging from the flag pole. One time we got some of the guy's shorts and wrote "bad" words on them with a permanent magic marker. They never came clean in the laundry. Here in college guys and girls live on the same floor and almost in the same room. The girl I was talking about thinks this freedom is great. Life is really different.

It has been a struggle for me in many areas but one of the first things I did was to find a church where I could find some kids who were wanting to please the Lord. It has been good to be with a group of Christians who really enjoy the Lord and know He is real in their lives. Some are from college but others just live here in town. People in the church have had me for dinner and invited me over just for fun. That has helped a lot. I am sure my parents would not have chosen this church but it sure is a big lift for me. They get kind of excited about the music and stuff but at least I don't feel like I am at a funeral every weekend.

One of the things that really bothers me is that a lot of people think because my parents are missionaries I must be here at college preparing to be a missionary. That is definitely not in my plans. Not that I am opposed to others going but because my parents are missionaries that doesn't mean I'll be one. I think it is so easy for MKs to be missionaries because they feel so out of it in their home county. The easiest thing to do is go back where they know the culture and the language. It seems to me that an MK needs a stronger call to missionary work than the average Christian because it is the easiest thing to do. I knew a lot of MKs who came back to the mission field because they couldn't do much else and that confirms my conviction.

I think I will make it. I can see I will not be very close to my parents now that I am in college. I have a scholarship for part of my expenses. They feel like they have done their job by getting me into college. I must make it on my own now. Some people have helped me and I am working part time to take care of the rest of the costs.

Yes the Lord has given me a lot of help. I have grown in my Christian life because of all I have gone through especially the last few years. I do want to live for the Lord. But I also want to catch up on the life I missed out on when my parents took me overseas. I missed knowing my grandparents. One died while I was in high school at boarding school. I always think of that and how much I miss him. He was a wonderful man. He was a great Christian. Another is so frail he is in a nursing home and doesn't even know me. The other one is so far away I may never get to really have time with her.

By the Lord's grace I can finish college, get a job as a teacher and settle down as a wife and mother in a suburban community that is like the one I left almost twenty years ago. Now it is time for me to find the will of God for my life. I hope I learned something from the experience my parents took me through. I am not bitter about it but it does seem like someone arranged my life for me without even asking me. I know some MKs that are very bitter. A few are really angry at God, and their parents and may never recover. I pray that will never happen to me. I know I cannot change the past but by the grace of God the future seems bright to me.

Sincerely,

PS: I really do thank the Lord for my wonderful parents.

Chapter 7

A Missionary on Furlough

Dear Special Friends,

It is time for us to return to the mission field after almost a year in the states. We left the field anticipating special goals which filled our minds and hearts. Most have not been fulfilled. Our hearts are discouraged and disappointed with the results of our time in the states. Sure we were tired when we packed all our things, but we were excited as we boarded a plane for home.

When we left our field we looked forward to many things that would make our year a very profitable experience for the whole family. The children would see the states as young adults instead of boys and girls. We would visit people who pray for us and support us. The excitement of sharing our ministry with groups of Christians all across the country was transparently evident. The need for a change of pace was all too obvious after the nonstop activity of the field. The possibility of interesting others in serving with us on this mission field was lodged firmly but prominently in our hearts. The task of purchasing supplies to take back with us was a part of the list we carried with us. Though we did not like to be away from our missionary work, it was the best thing to do. It was clear the Lord had directed our steps .

We are missionaries who have been on the field for more than twenty years. This is our fifth furlough and a very different one for sure. A fair amount of time had been spent writing to churches we wanted to visit or corresponding with key men in various areas of the country hoping to utilize our year as positively as possible. Several hurdles were overcome with relative ease such as purchasing a car for our travel, finding school books suitable for the children during the year, arranging for mail delivery, seeing about health appointments, and knowing where each part of the year would be spent. The Lord had clearly gone before us.

What we were not prepared for were the responses of so many people. We were unaware that the church was so illiterate in missions. On our previous furlough we were able to spend quality time with so many people and we had meetings in a significant number of churches. We encountered a keen interest in missions in general and our work in particular. We found missions conferences were well attended and carefully planned. We enjoyed the stay in the homes of many of the believers. It was a very positive experience for the whole family. That is why we approached our furlough with such wonderful anticipation.

As soon as we arrived in the states we immediately contacted the key individuals we were corresponding with about our day to day schedule. We were faced with a very apologetic summary of the reasons so few meetings were arranged in various metropolitan areas. They related how few assemblies had Sunday evening meetings, many churches have home study groups during the week in place of the mid-week prayer and Bible study. Others had only a handful at the prayer meeting so it would not be worth while to have a missionary report. The Sunday morning service was devoted to Bible teaching and so a missionary report would have to be limited to about ten minutes followed by a fifteen minute message. Sometimes just a ten minute report and nothing more. Some morning services were only 45 minutes in length! Some churches had pastors who did not want to interrupt the consecutive ministry. That was a hard adjustment when we are used to a meeting lasting about two or three hours since people walked for an hour or more to attend on the field.

When we began to piece together the schedule for the whole year we started to wonder why we came home on furlough at all! The whole schedule was arranged so that we had less than one meeting each week to share the burden of our work. We were faced with many days without any meetings at all! We were totally unprepared for the enormous change we found in assemblies and churches we felt we knew so well. How could it be that no one wrote to tell us things were so different from five years ago? Had people written and we had ignored the signs of the times? Our hearts sank as we considered the ramifications of spending this year at home. One thing was clear we would get a "rest" of sorts. With just a few meetings a week we would have to deal with a lot of "down time." The Lord must know we need this kind of "rest."

Our contacts further related to us that there were very few families who wanted to put missionaries up in their homes and so arrangements were being made for our accommodation in motels and apartments. It was not till the weeks began to unfold that we found ourselves sitting in motels day after day looking at each other wondering what we were doing there. We caught each other in tears on some occasions and on others just falling to our knees in prayer for the church. We found that the travel from place to place was no problem since the meetings were so few and far between. The lack of opportunity of personally visiting with people in their homes and talking about the work over a meal was one of the greatest sources of disappointment.

Our children had looked forward to getting to know other children in various homes with different families. Our children did enjoy the swimming pools at the motels but we found ourselves wanting to shield them from the disappointment we shared.

On several occasions we were in meetings but there was no opportunity for a message or a report. We were welcomed warmly and introduced as veteran missionaries. There was sincere appreciation for our visit. Why were we there? But we did want to be with the people of God even though we were not given opportunity to speak. On top of this we found the schedule for the church had been made up a year ago and there just wasn't any opportunity to insert a missionary speaker unless he spoke on the prearranged subject of the consecutive studies. We did enjoy that opportunity a couple of times but it did not leave any room for sharing our burden for missions. We might just as well have gone to our home church and stayed there for much of our furlough.

Our hearts were full of the work of the Lord but few places offered an outlet for information and a report. There wasn't even time for understanding questions about our work. People would ask where we were from, followed by "Where is that?" They asked about the weather in our country more than anything else. We were asked what we did, after the usual greeting "How are you?" It has been very frustrating to want to share for an hour or so what the Lord has done and know most people do not want answers any more than they want an answer to "How are you?"

We longed for serious discussion of missions and a substantial exchange in the Scriptures. We feel we have a lot to give. We hungered for in-depth teaching from the Bible. So much of what we heard and overheard was shallow teaching and discussion of sports, politics, and satisfying "our" needs. Our hearts are very heavy. This feeling will be a burden we carry till our next furlough. What will we do then?" It might seem carnal and unspiritual to mention this but with so few meetings the expenses of our furlough did not begin to be met by "fellowship" for speaking because we had so few. The costs of motels, gas, meals, tolls, car repairs, and the occasional "entertainment for the children" mounted up. Again we looked at each other and wondered how we would afford the cost of air tickets back to the field if we could hardly cover day to day expenses. We reminded ourselves that the Lord would provide and He has in amazing ways and from some of the strangest sources. Yes! we are serving a great God. We have encouraged ourselves in the Lord. When we did visit some assemblies we were amazed at the level of missionary interest.

It was not unusual for us to look for a missionary bulletin board or map to find out what missionaries were sent out or supported by each church. Again we were not prepared for the lack of interest in missionaries and the obvious failure to keep the people up to date on missionary activity. It was not unusual to find pictures of missionaries that were at least ten years old. I think the oldest picture on a bulletin board was close to 20 years. In the picture the children were about 3 or 4 years old and now they were just finishing college. Several pictures were of missionaries who were no longer on the field and a few were of missionaries who were in glory. I hope some of these missionaries do not come and find pictures of themselves that old. Some of the letters posted on the board were themselves over two years old. We wondered to ourselves if these sources of information were used to encourage people to pray. We found many people had never heard of the book Operation World as a guide to understanding the needs of world missions.

Occasionally we saw a copy of a financial report lying on a table for any one to take. We were faced again with the interesting, if not discouraging, relationship of giving to the needs of the church with the missions disbursements. We found a real lack of missionary support. Even locally commended workers were not regularly supported according to the annual financial report.

Obviously the greatest need we have as missionaries is prayer support. That was one of our greatest goals when we arrived almost a year ago. Several things cause us special concern in this regard. Without regular reports from missionaries in meetings and few opportunities afforded to read letters from missionaries the news is not getting to people and so their prayers for missions are very simplistic. We heard some of the prayers in the meetings and realized that the kind of spiritual intercession that is needed is almost nonexistent. Perhaps the problems and spiritual weakness we experience on the field is directly related to the lack of effectual prayer at home. Even the elders and leaders pray the same words one after the other.

Another source of disappointment is the lack of missionary conferences. During the year we have only attended four conferences directly related to missions. We asked what had happened over the five years and were told that many of the regional missionary conferences were canceled for lack of interest. With the demise of these meetings there was little opportunity to let people know that we needed laborers on the field. We had hoped to encourage several to become interested in our field of service and "Come over and help us." We return without a single prospect.

We are also concerned about the direction some of the mission agencies are taking that serve us. They seem to have lost touch with the changes that are taking place on the mission field. It is not the same as it was 40 years ago. Even 20 years has made a profound difference in methods and relationships with other mission agencies. Sometimes it is as if they do not understand what is going on where we are working. Their concept of a missionary is often colored by nostalgia or by special methodology. It is just not possible to sit under a palm tree and wait for people to come hear the gospel. We need to work with other members of the body of Christ as is mandated by the Scriptures themselves. Why do they have to be so sectarian and serve only the initiated or separate "those with us and those with them"? Many on our field are commended by assemblies just like we are but they are "not of us" and are not included. How can the nationals know the harmony of the Body of Christ when we do not even serve with missionaries sent from our own groups.

Yes! The year is up. Our children have survived, but they are keenly aware that our own emotions have been sadly shaken. The list of things we wanted to fulfill has fallen by the wayside as we faced repeated attitudes and actions that communicated a significant lack of interest and concern for missions. On our next furlough we will have the task of settling our children in college and we wonder how we should spend that time if the Lord has not come back for all of us.

I know that you did not expect to get a letter like this from a missionary, but I felt it was necessary to express our honest feelings. Most Christians are prepared for a report of success and fulfillment in the life and service of missionaries. If we were to share our disappointment and discouragement most would think us unfit for missionary service. But we return to the field knowing again that we are in the will of the Lord serving our faithful God and a spiritually hungry community called our mission field. We also know that we leave behind a church that has less and less interest in missions and very few opportunities to increase that interest.

Yes we need your prayers, and as we return we are thankful to you for your promise to pray for us regularly. Our feelings are mixed. We had such great hopes when we returned and leave with many of those hopes seriously damaged. Our hope is in the Lord whom we love and whom we serve. We are learning again that the Lord is absolutely trustworthy and we remain in His service, at His command for the salvation of a dying world.

Yours because we are His,

PS: I guess I should not write like this, but these thoughts have been simmering in my mind for a year. I cannot share these at a meeting or a conference because many would not understand. One of the special blessing we have had over the years is being able to open our hearts to you and know you still love us and make us feel useful. That has not been the case with many others who have cut us off when we did not toe the line they put in front of us. We are very human and have thoughts that cannot come to the surface because of the rejection we would experience. We know! And it hurts. Thanks for listening.

Chapter 8

A Missionary Mother

Dear Anne,

I am sorry to write this but I do not know what else to do. We have been on the mission field for twelve years and I still do not feel like a missionary. Everything I do I could do at home. But I would not be a missionary. Let me start from the beginning.

You remember when we were both little girls in church and the missionaries would come and show slides of their work. We talked all the time about being missionaries. It all seemed so exciting to us then and we knew the Lord would call us both to serve in some far away place. We both know it was girlish talk with a sprinkling of true spiritual devotion. We really hoped it would happen. We even talked once of never getting married and serving together as single "lady missionaries." Those were great dreams!

I remember so clearly the "old ladies" who came and talked to us in Sunday School about being missionaries. They seemed so old but they did describe a wonderful service to the Lord. As I look back I think it might have been better to have stayed single and be a missionary. I really felt a call from those two.

But you know what happened. We went off to different colleges and of course each met our Mr. Wonderful! You and Ben have done so well over the 15 years you have been married. You have everything we talked about as little girls when we weren't talking about being missionaries. You remember the things we wanted in a man and in life? You have a lovely home. Ben has a good job. You have a car and a mini-van, a boat and lots of vacation time. Your life seems so perfect. You have your two children and all the things they want you can provide. You don't have to work and can spend so much time with them. Anne, I really am jealous!

But then I think of what the Lord called us to do. Joe is such a good father and we have four wonderful children but here we are out in the bush and my mind goes back to our childhood so often. I know it is not right to think like this but the vision of missionary work I saw when I was young and even when we got married has been shattered.

I remember when I really truly surrendered to be a missionary. God was doing business and I was doing business. I meant it. I was available to the Lord to serve wherever and whenever He chose. I committed myself to the job of being a missionary. Joe did exactly the same thing. We used to talk of it when we were dating. The picture of us serving the Lord together filled our every thought. We made all our decisions of life based on being missionaries. We could not think of anything else. We did not even have the thoughts I have now. We did not even look at cars and houses and things like that. This was before we got married.

Joe was such a great personal worker and I really felt the Lord called me to teach Bible studies to the women. I did everything I could to prepare for the job of filling my days with preparing Bible study materials, leading Bible studies, having a lot of women to disciple, talking to women about life, marriage, children, the church and the home. I could not have been more dedicated or filled with preparing for the vocation of being a missionary.

Joe too was really involved with developing his gift to do personal work. He was not a great preacher when we met, but he tried to improve it and he does really well now. He was such a wonderful person to talk to and so easy to relate to. I guess that is why I loved him so much and we decided we would make a great team. What wonderful days those were.

We got married after college and our every thought was to get to the mission field as soon as possible. The Lord had called it was clear. We devoted our every effort to getting prepared. We went back home as a married couple and began to make all the arrangements to go. The Lord did not have to speak very loud to tell us where to go. We agreed right away. We had no doubts. Our church was so great in sending us. We look back and realize that our dream had come true. The dream we used to talk about as girls. The dream Joe and I planned for.

You have been wonderful to us too. I can never forget the encouragement you gave us all along the way. The four of us, you and Ben and me and Joe such great friends. We left with your blessing and prayers. We never thought about where you might go, what you might do or how you would live. We all, I think, were happy with the way the Lord guided us all. It seemed perfect for you and for us. Your interest in missions was always there even though the Lord did not call you overseas.

We had such wonderful times when we first arrived. We laughed and talked about everything and found so many things funny beyond belief. We did not write because no one would believe us if we did write. The food we had to eat was a scream. The snakes and bugs were all around. You and I would have had a ball laughing and talking all night. Joe and I had awesome experiences those first years. I would not trade them for all the world.

I wish the story did not change! It hasn't for you. You have your family and it was always such good news when we heard you had a child and then another. What a perfect family!

For me the story is very different even though it may surprise you. When we were home on furlough I had to play the role of a missionary's wife. Our children had to be good. We were on display and I could not talk to anyone about the feelings that have been building up. I must have looked so pious and holy.

Let me talk. You are the only one I can write. How I wish you were here to talk to.

When we settled in here I began to fulfill the dreams of a lifetime. We were serving together just as we planned. Joe was involved right away learning the language and I was trying to have some Bible studies with my limited vocabulary. But I was working on it.

We decided to have children before we were married very much longer. So Bill came along and brought such joy. Then Janice and then the twins. Boy did that change my life! And that seems to be the root of the problem.

I felt so fulfilled doing what the Lord had called me to do. Studying, teaching, counseling, and visiting filled my every day. I could not have been happier. Now I do not have time enough to have my own quiet time. I do not know the language. I can't seem to understand the culture. All I do is take care of kids. My every waking moment is spent in taking care of the children and my husband. I know it is terrible even to think it but I never envisioned myself in this situation. Of course we would have children. For some reason I thought I could do both. Remember we used to talk about it as girls. But I never realized I would have to stop being a "missionary" because I have children. I know that sounds terrible but that is how I feel.

What is so annoying is that Joe is still fulfilling his dream. He is out every day talking to people, seeing them saved, encouraging them, visiting with them, learning the language, teaching them. People say he talks just like one of the nationals. Everything he came to do he is doing. Everything I came to do I am not doing. We are not missionaries. Joe is and I am not. I hardly know a dozen sentences of the language. I have forgotten most of what I learned and the only real contact I have is with the house girl.

When little Billy came into our family he brought such joy and fulfillment. We prayed for him and dedicated him to the Lord. We did the same with Janice. I guess we were not prepared for twins.

We were really quite pleased with just a boy and a girl. But the Lord gave them to us. They are darling and we love them to pieces but I am not doing missionary work. As the family grew I found myself doing nothing but feeding, washing, clothing, cleaning, reading, playing, teaching, and correcting my four children. I can do all of this at home and do it much easier and the children would have a much better life. I often ask myself when I am alone, "What am I doing here? I might as well come home and take care of the kids and let Joe be the missionary."

Yes, it is putting a strain on our relationship as well. Joe is always coming back home for lunch and telling me of all the exciting things he's been doing. New words he learned. New concepts of the language that help him share the gospel. All the new contacts he has. Every day is new to him. And I have no way of relating to that ministry. Dirty noses, dirty clothes, dirty house, dirty feet, and a dirty heart. My dirty heart is the worst thing I have. I feel like such a hypocrite.

When he is home he talks about Sorona his secretary. He eats lunch and heads back to the office where Sorona is typing and filing. That does not sit well in my imagination. I get so tired of hearing her name I could scream. Then he is off to visit some people in the afternoon and comes back to the office to close up.

Even last year when we were home on furlough I felt like such a hypocrite when we showed our slides of the work and I just stood there like a beautiful wall picture. What people thought and what I was thinking were very different. Everything was about what Joe was doing, he is preaching, teaching, sharing, discipling, visiting and on and on. What was I doing? Nothing but taking care of the kids. A lovely picture of the kids and us. What a wonderful family serving the Lord every one would think. I would be seething and boiling over. Glad to be back home but so dirty, looking like a saint at church but knowing I did not consider myself a missionary.

I was a maid, a cook, a teacher, a mother, a laundry servant, a house girl but certainly not a missionary. I was no different than the girl who did some of the dishes and washing up except she was probably not overflowing with anger and envy. But surely she knew what I was thinking. The nationals know us better then we know ourselves. I can tell by her words that she knows what I am thinking. The folk back home are not as good at discerning our minds and we can fool them a lot of the time. But on the field they know our every thought.

What can I do? I feel I cannot go on like this. I cannot admit my feelings to anyone but you. Joe would not understand and if I told him he would not know what to do. Going home is out of the question since we would be failures. The weight of that failure would be too much for me. I could not live with that the rest of my life. But I cannot live like this either. I am the one that is failing not Joe. I am the one who would bring us home. I am the one who could not handle the culture or whatever we decided was the reason for coming home.

Yes, my health is not good. But it is not my health physically but spiritually. The relation between the two is so close. I know that my physical problems are all generated by the emotional and spiritual battles I have every day. My health was the reason for quitting the ladies Bible classes and other things that keep me in the missionary loop. But I know it all goes back to the struggle within.

Anne, I have never written a letter like this to any one else, but I had to tell someone. I do not know what you can do for me, but I would appreciate a letter or something to help me out of this morass I find myself in.

With very special love,

PS: I guess I did not even ask you to pray for me. You know I need prayer. But I do not need the kind of prayers we hear all the time at home on furlough "Lord bless, be with, guide, direct and protect the missionaries." I need help! Thanks for listening. I love you so much!

PPS: Say Hi to your kids and to Ben. I am constantly thinking of you and your family.

Chapter 9

"Shipwrecked" Missionaries

Dear Family of God,

We have shipwrecked our lives, disappointed our family, failed the church which sent us out, dishonored the friends who supported us, caused the world to blaspheme the name we profess to serve, jeopardized the faith of those we were serving on the field, were tempted to show that failure is all right if you are Christians, and caused the body of Christ unnecessary pain and suffering. Above all we disgraced the Lord Jesus Christ our God.

We blame no one but ourselves. We do not accuse each other but take the responsibility for the shipwreck equally. We did not attend to the ship of our life as we are commanded in the scriptures. We did not practice what we preached. We did not check the set of our sails. We did not honor what we committed ourselves to when we went out as missionaries. We did not provide maintenance for our ship. We were insensitive to the ministry of the Holy Spirit. We rationalized our activities because we were so busy. We accepted that the work of the Lord must come ahead of every other thing in our lives. The only thing we could do was come home to repair and reconcile our lives and not abandon the ship all together.

We were guilty of adultery. We say "we" because when we committed ourselves to each other in marriage the minister said from the Word of God that "we are made one" and "Therefore what God has joined together, let not man separate." We firmly believed, in the newness of our relationship, that we were bound together and were willing to go through anything and everything as if we were one for as long as we lived. We delighted in that ecstasy and joy of really "living" as one. We were convinced that nothing could come between us or force us not take equal responsibility for whatever happened in our lives and service for the Lord. We never imagined this kind of storm for our ship.

Most who experience what we have put ourselves through do not write this kind of a letter. They quietly come home, find another community, another church, other friends and very often other ships and shipmates. This is not an option as far as we can see from a simple reading of the Word of God. It is our duty to "Confess your trespasses to one another, and pray for one another, that you may be healed." Yes, we need healing. But all too often the tragic shipwreck we have survived is cause for boarding another ship with another mate and setting out on the waters of life "better prepared to help others" because of what we have been through. It is our conviction that we need to be healed and because we are healing we can perhaps help others.

When we were married we were fully committed believers and had the whole hearted desire to serve the Lord wherever He might call us. To be missionaries was a very real option and we tried to set our sails in the direction of some foreign country where we might be able to serve unloved and unreached people with the gospel.

The Lord did call us and we prepared ourselves as best we could to go out into all [at least one country] the world and make disciples. We chose under the Lord's help a "ship" that we thought was right for the voyage to a country where we would be well suited for service knowing our gifts and abilities. We left our shores and sailed [by air] with our two young children and headed for a fulfilling vision of "serving the Lord." Our church was fully behind us and gave us the "right hand of fellowship." Many friends gave sacrificially for our "passage" and the equipment we would need for our missionary work. We felt we were prepared for service because of our training, our vocations, our experience and devotion to the Lord. Like many missionaries we were committed for the long voyage. This was not a pleasure cruse or a round the world trip to see if it was for us. It was a one way ticket on a merchant ship that was designed for rough waters and permanent service whatever the cost.

We arrived filled with hope and awareness of the huge task the Lord had given us. We had been "filled in" by other missionaries about some of the pitfalls and traps of service in this part of the "vineyard." It was not without a fair amount of apprehension we launched into language study and cultural assimilation in a totally new world.

It was trying in many ways to form new words in our mouth, accept that people were always going to be gawking at us, realize that people did not appreciate the sacrifice we had made to go there, and learn new ways of shopping, cooking, and eating. It was frustrating not to be able to get our ideas across, not to be accepted by other missionaries because we are from a different country, not to have our opinions considered in decisions, not to understand the Bible as others do, and not even to think as other missionaries think.

Many nights we would fall into bed with the special consolation that at least we had each other and that in the quietness of the night no one could come between us. We held each other close in the narrow bed but we were so close we did not need a king-size bed to spread out on. We loved being close and were glad it was necessary in these primitive conditions. Those were very special times that we relished and savored. The next day always dawned brighter and we could get up and face the trials of missionary "orientation" even though it was not a formal curriculum.

As a result of "being close" we had two more children in fairly quick succession. They were the joy of our life as were the others the Lord gave us before we arrived on the field. The addition of two more made some changes in our life. We shifted responsibilities as we adjusted to more demands on our energies, our time, our resources and our spiritual commitment to a rigorous schedule of activities.

There were some activities that (Now we have a problem because we are almost forced to separate our activities between what he does and what she does. This makes it very hard to write this letter together and accept responsibility for all that happened equally. But we cannot continue without realizing that we are forced to accept, we were doing different things all the time, but they did not seem important in the overall picture of accountability to each other. Obviously for our whole married life we did separate things and different things. But in this letter we want to guard the biblical premise; we are both guilty of the shipwreck that we have caused. Thanks for trying to understand.) needed to be done by him and others that needed to be done by her at least because of the increased family.

I [she] spend long hours up many nights trying to help children through malaria, lonesomeness, colds, the flu, common childhood diseases and many other sleepless times. I [he] had so many pressing duties with the building of a mission work, teaching Bible classes, discipling young men, opening an office and organizing a host of details that would make the work develop smoothly. We hired a gardener so that I [she] would be free to give more time to the children but also so I [she] would be able to teach some ladies Bible classes, teach sewing, give literacy classes, teach hygiene and give out simple medicines. I [he] found the demands of the office so overwhelming that we needed to hire an office girl. She could do typing, filing, data entry, and a host of reports that are needed to have a handle on what is happening. She would need hours of training on the computer, teaching the filing system, explaining the office procedure and handling dozens of requests that came to the office door every day.

By now we had finished with the long hours of language training, and felt like we had adjusted to the culture somewhat.

We had been home for one furlough and were considering another but had not yet made the decision when to go. We moved from the very cramped quarters that we lived in during our first term. Many things changed so slowly we did not recognize the differences that were transforming our ministry and our lives. A little office was built so we could move a lot of things out of the house and give us more room. We did not have such a small home now so we were able to have a bigger kitchen table and some cabinets built. We had some living room chairs made and a bookcase. We were able to afford to have a chest of drawers and a bed built for each of the children. In fact we had a bigger bed built for ourselves and gave our old one to our first child.

As we look back on the easing of pressure in one area we now realize the pressure was building in another. We seldom had the times of falling into bed and into each other's arms as we had done half a dozen years ago. We went to bed at different times, we got up at different times because of different demands, different projects and schedules. Our new big bed did allow us to "spread out" and not have the contact we had enjoyed so much before. We often found the next day began as the last had finished; with the burden unlifted because it had not been shared. Because we had such different ministries and activities we slowly flowed in different directions.

One of us would fall into bed very desirous of some special attention or relief of some muscle ache or back pain. But the other was asleep or too tired. We found we did not share our problems or our joys. We found that we were living more and more apart. Sharing fewer and fewer special moments.

We both felt it was the Lord's work we were doing and commitment to that service was what we were there for, so we must accept that these changes will come. I [she] trusted that the pressure would ease off when the office girl learned all she needed to learn. I [he] trusted that as the children grew older she (here again we are at an impasse. It must be said that we looked at each other and wondered if the life complications were not the fault of the other's busyness, and that an adjustment in the other's schedule would smooth out the roughness in our relationship. Though we did look at each other like that we accept equal and full responsibility for the shipwreck we allowed. I hope you will try to understand.) would have more time to devote to me. (again, to say "Me" is to isolate one from the other and suggest that we were not one. It was when we began to look at ourselves as the lacking party that the trouble began. This is the root of the problem as we are learning to sort it out in the midst of this healing. Please try to understand.)

As we failed to meet each others needs we both found a hearing ear in someone other than the one we had committed ourselves to so many years ago when we said "I do!" The gardener was learning English and I [she] was learning his language. We (now for the first time we are using the word "we" to refer to someone other than our mates. This is a small fly in the ointment of our relationship but still causes a stink) shared the problems of life, life in the village with a family, problems of being a foreigner in a foreign country and a host of things that made life unfulfilling. During this time it was convenient to expose the failure of others as the reason for the strain of our relationship.

I [he] found a convenient ear in the office girl who was always there and I [he] found I [he] was spending more time in the office with urgent duties than at home with pressing problems. The gulf grew. We both failed to deal with our feelings and thoughts. They were seemingly too private to even talk about since we were not sharing much else in our relationship. Opportunities were available while I [he] was at the office and while I [she] was teaching Bible classes at the church. It all became very fuzzy and we rationalized our feelings and thoughts in the seclusion of our own minds.

Yes, we committed adultery! Which of us? This is a question that everyone seems to want to know. The answer is there as far as the world and even most Christians is concerned. But as far as the Lord, the Scriptures and ourselves, we both did. Not the physical act necessarily! But our commitment was not fulfilled as we promised each other, the witnesses of our marriage and above all the Lord God. We know that this is unsatisfactory to most believers because we all want to "pin the sin on the guilty party." We are the guilty party! If we isolate one of us as the "guilty party" then the other is set free by the world and many in the church to jump ship, board another and sail out of the other's life leaving them to commiserate in their own abyss.

Of course we were shocked when it was discovered by each other, by the church, by the community, by our children. Our lives were in the turmoil of anger, guilt, frustration, shame, humiliation, embarrassment, and many other emotions and temptations about solving the personal hurt. The shock reached our home church, supporting friends and many others in churches near and far from our home. We learned death is often easier than this. The weeks that followed included talking, shouting, explaining to the children, walking, weeping, confessing, praying, reading and wishing we were dead.

The decision to leave the field was one of the first we made. That meant we had to dispose of a lot of things, pack others, sell what we could, give some away, and make arrangement for ministries and jobs. Purchasing air tickets and planning a departure from a family of believers we had deeply hurt and failed miserably was not an easy task. The whole experience at times overwhelmed us and drove us to each other. On other occasions it drove us so far apart we wondered if we knew each other.

The children were hurt through no fault of their own. They had to explain to their friends, leave school, gather things to help their memories, pack a few toys or keepsakes and say good-by to special people. The pain in their lives continues with scars that will be uncovered from time to time as they make their way through life. They found it satisfying to blame one of us rather than both. We needed to teach them that as believers there is no alternative to pressing on in search of healing such as saying "I quit." This learning experience is for them almost as hard as for us.

It was a relief to get on the plane and be with a group of people who did not know what had happened. But we knew it was a short respite since we would be met at the airport near our home town by people who knew. We would then be faced by a community of family and friends who would have a whole array of emotional reactions and who would place blame and give solutions to both of us how it should be handled.

There were many who came to us lamenting the work of the devil in our relationship. This has produced a temptation to confusion when the Word of God is clear about the source of fulfilling the "desires of the flesh." Even "Christians" wanted to suggest another source. The Bible is transparent that the kind of sin we were guilty of comes from within our own selves. James 1:13-16 says, "Let no one say when he is tempted, "I am tempted by God"; for God cannot be tempted by evil, nor does He Himself tempt anyone. But each one is tempted when he is drawn away by his own desires and enticed. Then, when desire has conceived, it gives birth to sin; and sin, when it is full-grown, brings forth death. Do not be deceived, my beloved brethren."

It is instructive that James concludes his identification of the real source of such sin by saying "Do not be deceived . . ." It is so much easier for us to blame each other for the failure of meeting our needs and so deceive ourselves. It is one of the devil's tricks to tempt us to think that he is responsible for sin that comes from within us. To blame the other is to excuse our own failure and give the impression that the other is free because of the "innocent party" idea. To blame the devil is to attempt to set us both free from the guilt. Our minds were often confused by the cacophony of advice from so many well meaning people. The silent treatment was painful coming from some dear friends. The pastoral counsel was simplistic and unrealistic for the longed for healing. We chose healing because our God is a healing God. We are convinced that the Lord is glorified far more through the healing process than through selfish searching for human happiness in a new relationship.

We chose healing as a means of proving God's faithfulness in this circumstance of life. We are learning what the Lord means when He says: "For I am the LORD who heals you" (Exodus 15:25). "Who forgives all your iniquities, Who heals all your diseases" (Psalm 103:3). "He sent His word and healed them, And delivered them from their destructions" (Psalm 107:20). "He heals the brokenhearted, And binds up their wounds" (Psalm 147:3).

We were strongly reminded that God chose to bring reconciliation with Himself to us instead of starting all over with a new race of people. He also chooses to bring reconciliation to His children if they will believe Him and obey His word. What a contradiction it would be for God to reconcile the whole world to Himself and have no plan to reconcile His children to each other. Can it be that reconciliation of His children is beyond His power? Or are His children unwilling to accept His power but rather go on their own way of selfishness? The cost of reconciling the world was His Son. The cost of reconciling us to each other is the same. We chose reconciliation!

Of course the healing process is taking a long time and is painful. But the injury time was long and painful. We had "friends" abandon us as we were trying to work through the scriptures finding the healing the Lord promises to all who seek it. We also gained new friends who have helped immensely in recovering our social and spiritual health. Some in the family of God have been like cheerleaders as we fought our way back to normalcy in our fellowship with the Lord, ourselves, the church and the world.

We were encouraged to go ahead and get a divorce by "Christian" friends and get on with our lives. But as we searched the scriptures we learned; "For the LORD God of Israel says, That He hates divorce, For it covers one's garment with violence" (Malachi 2:16). Equally clear is the teaching that to remarry is to compound the problem. "So then if, while her husband lives, she marries another man, she will be called an adulteress; but if her husband dies, she is free from that law, so that she is no adulteress, though she has married another man" (Romans 7:3). "But even if she does depart, let her remain unmarried or be reconciled to her husband. And a husband is not to divorce his wife." "A wife is bound by law as long as her husband lives; but if her husband dies, she is at liberty to be married to whom she wishes, only in the Lord" (1 Corinthians 7:11, 39).

Some who had been through divorce and remarriage came to us with very conflicting counsel. How can the Lord lead equally "devoted" believers in such opposite ways? we asked. To follow man's message would have brought us to conclude that the Lord is not the Healer but the "Helper" to find another ship going a different direction. This we did not believe. Some said it was like heaven to begin again. Others said it was like hell. The Lord gave us "Cease ye from man, whose breath is in his nostrils" (Isaiah 2:22).

We were challenged by the many times God says "He is able . . ." Divorce says "I quit," says "God can't help," says "I won't let God do it in me." We believe He is able!

We are healing. We are finding the Lord is adequate for this tragedy of our life. We know we may have disqualified ourselves for some ministries. So why write this letter which no one else writes. Because the God of all comfort "comforts us in all our tribulation, that we may be able to comfort those who are in any trouble, with the comfort with which we ourselves are comforted by God." There is a ministry the Lord has given us. Helping to bring healing to a segment of our Christian society who are tempted to think that God is more interested in our being happy than in our being healed. We have found that those who seek happiness do not find healing. But those who seek healing find happiness.

We have re-established our home near where we lived before being called as missionaries. Our family is finding its place in a community that desperately needs to have a window into the great grace of our wonderful God. We are in a church where we are loved, and where we are beginning to find a place of usefulness.

We have given ourselves to each other again on this our 15th anniversary of saying "I do." We come first in each other's life as 1 Corinthians 7:32 teaches us, "But I want you to be without care. He who is unmarried cares for the things of the Lord—how he may please the Lord. But he who is married cares about the things of the world—how he may please his wife."

Yes, many in the world know who did it. But as far as God and we are concerned, we were guilty. Because of this confession we are healing. I [he] have a job that by the Lord's goodness meets our financial needs. I [she] am finding the greatest calling in the world, "motherhood," a special challenge. Our children need us more than ever. The children are developing a healthy view of marriage and the family as we all learn together "He gives more grace." Therefore He says: "God resists the proud, But gives grace to the humble. Therefore submit yourselves to God. Resist the devil and he will flee from you. Draw near to God and He will draw near to you. Cleanse your hands, you sinners, and purify your hearts, you double-minded" (James 4:6).

Healing is always a long process. There is the itch and pain of the skin as it recovers from some gash. The urge to peal off the scab and open the wound extends and slows the healing process. There is the need to learn to walk after a broken leg. But it takes a strong will to return a broken bone to usefulness. But healing is possible.

In a shipwreck it is a marvel when everyone does not abandoned ship and save themselves. To almost go down with the ship and then know ". . . underneath are the everlasting arms . . ." raising a wreck to be reconditioned, renewed and recommissioned for use is to experience the miracle of our great God who also said "He will thrust out the enemy from before you . . ." (Deuteronomy 33:27). Join us in thanking the Lord for His healing and the boldness to believe that He is a God of reconciliation and restoration.

Healing and happy,

PS: We now have a narrow bed!

Chapter 10

A Retired Missionary

Dear Partners in His Service,

I am home after a lifetime of service to the Lord in the deepest jungle. I can look back on over 45 years of service to one of the most remote tribes of the world. We left after a fulfilling work satisfied that we had done all we could to provide the gospel in the language of the people, establish churches, and train evangelists. There are several churches carrying on just as we set them up. There is a simple medical work, a school for elementary children and a short term Bible school for evangelists.

But now we are home. I say home but it doesn't seem like home anymore. Things have changed so much in those fifty years. My heart sinks when I see the church I left importing the world to please the people. The music is different, the preaching shallow, the fashions obscene, the practices questionable, the attendance skimpy, the offerings meager, the prayers monotonous, the worship superficial, and activities are secular. I wonder what I am going to do. Why did I come home from the field?

When I was a foreign missionary it was a joy to go around and share the work of the Lord to our churches. People seemed so interested and positive about our activities and ministries.

Many asked what they could do, how they could pray, what we needed, what were our plans for the future and what the needs were on the field. But now I am home. No one asks any questions about anything. I feel so used up and unneeded. I still try to keep up with the many things that are going on in the field but no one seems interested. I used to be asked to speak and give reports but now I have no invitations to speak and no reports to give. You can only show your slides of the work so many times. Have I just come home to die?

When I was on the mission field there were a hoard of leaders, elders, evangelists, pastors and teachers at my door hungry for teaching and instruction. Many came asking questions regarding the Scriptures and their application in the church, in the family, and in life. We discussed problems in the churches and knotty theological issues. But now I am home and it seems no one comes to visit, no one asks my advice or values the wisdom of over 40 years experience on the mission field. No one calls to ask my thoughts on a portion of scripture or how to deal with a problem in the church. I'm never invited to sit with the elders and so do not really even know what is happening in my home church.

One of the delights of my life on the field was the mail. At first it only came every few weeks then regularly each Thursday, and in the last few years we got mail several times a week. It was a very special part of our ministry to answer letters. Both my wife and I were dedicated to correspond with any who were interested enough to write. We acknowledged every gift as soon as possible. We sent personal letters as a response to every personal letter. It was part of our ministry. But now I am home. Most times I come back from the mail box empty handed except for the "junk." Once a month we get the check from the government which allows us to carry on. We are not so frail that we cannot write but whom shall we write, except a few missionaries on the field and some family.

We don't often even have someone to talk to at home. The phone seldom rings and few stop to speak at church. I remember when the whole day was spent talking to people. At the end of the day I felt exhausted just from personal conversation. I suppose I wanted some peace then but not this kind of deathly silence! How I long for someone to talk to about something that really matters. How I wish the phone would ring and someone would ask how we are doing and what we are doing. But then I was so glad we didn't have a phone on the mission station and we talked to every one eye to eye. But now I am home.

The little apartment where we live now is so small compared to the large house on the station. It was always full of people coming and going. A steady stream of visitors coming at meal times. The food was always more than adequate because strangers as well as friends regularly showed up at meal times. The joy around the table, the fellowship in the things of the Lord, and the bountiful meal concluded with a Bible reading and prayer at the end. But now it hardly seems necessary to fix more than one meal a day. Few come by for even a cup of tea. And of course it is a very unusual thing to be invited out for a meal to someone else's house. We have had a meal or two but the days of fun and laughter around a loaded table are past.

Now we sit together for breakfast which is very simple, tea and toast. Then we read for a while, have mid-morning tea and then wait for lunch. We may go for a walk if the weather is nice. After lunch we take a nap and then it is time for the mail. Most times the mail is not worth going to the curb for. Once a week we go shopping and get a few things that are on sale. After supper we relax and read again before going to bed. Sunday is the only day that is different, and it is not always restful since we get so upset by what our church is doing.

Our children are not near. Their days are filled with many activities that leave little time for us. They come by for a visit on their way somewhere else and always want the grandchildren to know who we are. But we do not know who they really are. We get a little card from some of them as thanks for a birthday or Christmas gift which we send out of our meager living. Church, friends, ministry, family all gone and here we sit.

We do try to take a walk occasionally but it is not safe, many people tell us. We do give out a tract as we can and greet the neighbors warmly but no one has time to talk. We do not have any "hobbies." How can you have hobbies when your whole life is absorbed in serving the Lord overseas? The television is there, but most of what is on is obscene and even the news reviews the sorry condition of our world.

We often wish the Lord would come and take us home. But we know that His time is not always the same as ours. We bask in the words "To be absent from the body is to be present with the Lord." But we know we should not want the Lord to come just to get us out of this mess. We should really want Him to come because we love Him so much. I am thinking of going back to the mission field. That is some place where I am needed and wanted. I remember spending a lot of time preparing messages for the Lord's people. The meetings would go on all afternoon and then there were long discussions with various ones. People walked for hours to come and really wanted to be taught. The appreciation was overwhelming as the hunger for the Word was so enjoyable to satisfy. These poor people would give a few eggs, a pumpkin, sometimes a chicken, or just a warm handshake. It was so fulfilling and satisfying.

But I do not want to be a burden and here at home I am not a burden to anyone. On the field I might get sick or fall and break a bone. Maybe it sounds like I am pitying myself and I guess I am. But I want to be useful. It is hard to get home and come to a dead stop. It would be easier to die on the field. I am ashamed I feel this way, but with so little activity my mind does not have many curbs. I didn't intend to write a letter like this, but, well, Yes. We are people too and we need your prayers.

Your faithful servant,

PS: Forgive me if I seem ungrateful for all the years the Lord has given me. It seems easier to look back than to look forward.

Chapter 11

A Failed Missionary

Dear Friends,

I tried missionary work and failed. I went out to serve the Lord but am now at home looking for a job. My call to missionary service was dramatic and specific. I took my family and left my parents to serve the Lord and give myself to people who had very little materially and nothing spiritually. I am disillusioned, discouraged with missionary service and disappointed with myself. How could this have happened to us? We had so much to give! We sacrificed so much! We lost so much! We understand so little!

Let me go back and summarize my missionary experience. When I was a young man I was in a meeting where a call for missionaries was presented. I knew the Lord was calling me to serve Him in a remote part of the world. A place where there were not many missionaries and where the commodities and amenities of the United States were nonexistent. I felt that the best service I could render to these people, whoever they were, was in the medical field. I set my sights on this goal to be a medical doctor. I dreamed of helping people while sharing the gospel with them. I left college with a premed. curriculum solidly under my belt and headed to medical school. It was not easy but the vision of opening a clinic and dispensing medicine kept me going. My church fellowship was spasmodic since I was heavily involved in medical school. While there God brought Betsy into my life. I shared my commitment and goal to serve the Lord in some remote part of the world in the medical field. Betsy was a nurse and our vision was mutual and we sensed the Lord had confirmed that we should serve the Lord as a team. We married just before I finished medical school and we longed to leave the shores of the USA for wherever the need was greatest.

With my internship finished I joined a private practice and began to get some hands-on experience which I felt would make my missionary life more practical. We now had three children and our debt for med. school was just about paid off. We began to pray about where the Lord wanted us to use our medical skills. We met missionaries, corresponded with them, talked to mission boards and began to envision exactly what it was we were prepared to do as missionaries. The Lord led us to serve in a very undeveloped country. We were encouraged by friends and family as well as reports of the great need for medical help in this remote part of the world. Missionaries were thrilled we were going.

I must tell you that we set out for the field with our children, our simple possessions, our skills, and a sense of the great sacrifice we were making to serve the Lord. The travel to the field was punctuated with outbursts of joy that we were going to serve the Lord overseas. At times we could hardly contain ourselves as we reviewed the way the Lord has led, provided, encouraged and protected us all along the way. The anticipation of the welcome we would receive was a muted sense of satisfaction of what we had given up to be here.

The missionary community was glad to see us. They had prayed for years that the Lord would send a medical doctor. We were here. After a few days of getting adjusted to the new time zone and taking care of many aspects of living, we were off in a small plane with our possessions and family to the interior. As the plane slipped onto the little airstrip we viewed hundreds of people waiting for us to arrive. They seemed excited beyond words. We got our things together and these happy people took our bags, boxes, suitcases and trunks to a waiting truck. The crowd melted away as we left on a slow rocky journey that seemed to toss the truck and its contents mercilessly from one side to the other of the cramped cab. We arrived at nightfall to a little cottage which would be our home for the next several years. Our things were unloaded and the old pick-up truck rattled its way down our path and out of sight. We had arrived.

We began the task of making living possible in the "cottage" which we found out did not have electricity, running water, or "facilities." The first day people came with gifts of bananas, squash, beans and many other expressions of their delight at having us there. We found people always watching us. Peering in our windows. Sitting near our house. Standing by the out-house. Staring at us as we walked around the little mission station. Following us to the market. Asking if they could carry things for us. Begging for gifts. Betsy, who is a very private person, found this very uncomfortable. The village children were at our house when we woke up and when we blew out the lanterns at night they were watching us. We had no privacy. As we learned a few words, we tried to get the folk to let us live in peace. A struggle began in us. We had come to serve, not to live in a fishbowl. We had no life of our own. The girl who worked for us in the house must have told every one in the village all about our life, our possessions and habits.

When the clinic opened at 8:00 AM there would be about 75 people with medical problems waiting for my attention. If I went out at 6:30 AM, just after I got up, there would only be about 25 but by 7:30 there were at least fifty. I fought with the idea of going to the hospital at 7:00 so that I would not have so many patients at 8:00 AM. I wanted to share the gospel with each one through the nursing assistant who translated the verses. But if I took a few minutes with each patient by noon I would only have seen about 25 – 30 and there would be about 175 more waiting when I came back from lunch. At the end of the day I would only have seen half the people that came to the clinic. They would have to walk home the 3-5 miles and start out long before dawn the next day to get to the clinic early so I could see them. If I did not talk to anyone about the Lord or the Christian life I would be able to see almost all the patients that came that day. The harder I tried the more confusing it became to me. I had prepared for this for more than ten years and now I was not able to talk to many about the gospel day after day.

In order to see the increased number of patients that were coming I began opening the clinic earlier, taking a shorter lunch time and staying open until I saw the last one. I could hardly bear the thought of a person walking 5 miles to see me and then be turned away at the end of the clinic hours without help. I had to see every one! When I got up in the morning I found that I looked out my window and saw the people already at the door of the clinic. I formed a habit of not eating breakfast so I could get to the clinic earlier. I even stopped having my quiet time so that I would be at the hospital sooner.

The things at the hospital got worse as well. I began to do surgery I had never been trained for. I saw some of the most amazing medical situations. My training never prepared me for what I was seeing regularly. We lost a few patients and I wondered why? How can I have come so far from home and still not be able to save a life. We did not have the equipment that was necessary to save some of the very ill. "If only we had . . ." I would say many times. We had a generator but we only used it at night for a hour or so. Even if we had the equipment we could not afford to use the generator all the time.

A number of other things were affected by this conflict. My children saw less of me. My attitude was changing. I began to resent the patients. My fuse blew more often. We didn't seem to have enough medicines. I lost my desire to share the gospel even if I did have time. I wrote very few letters. I did not have time for family devotions let alone prayer time with my wife. I was being defeated at the very core of my dream. Betsy was fully occupied with the house, schooling the children, having ladies meetings and a host of other little things that are expected of a missionary wife. She was frustrated with the fact that all her nurses training had not begun to be used on the mission field. Had all her training been for nothing? Were all the years of nursing going to be wasted on her children?

Betsy was frustrated with missionary life and service. Nobody told her how it was going to be. She felt the missionary community that recruited her had betrayed her. This is not the fulfillment of her dream of missionary work. We had very little time to discuss our feelings.

The leaders of the church began to expect a lot more from me as a missionary. The more I tried to do medically the more they wanted from me in the church. I found I could not begin to balance the enormous load that was on my shoulders. The more the elders of the church wanted from me the less I could do. They didn't seem to understand the sacrifice I made to be a missionary doctor in their community. It didn't dawn on them the amount of money I could be making back home under ideal conditions. I was a doctor on the missionfield, which very few were. Almost anyone could preach, teach or disciple new believers. "I can't do it all." I complained!

After two and a half years I began to feel so tired and exhausted I wondered if my health was failing. The need was so great! The sick seemed to be without number. Surely the Lord would give me good health. I couldn't stop seeing people who were so sick and had traveled so far. So many had encouraged me. Dozens were praying for us. People were giving to support us on the field. I found I just could not get up as early as I had. I needed more sleep. How could it not be working out? What should I do? I was completely exhausted physically, emotionally and did not know what I was spiritually.

By the time we had been there three years I realized that I could not continue. The arguments that reverberated in my mind were deafening. If I stayed I could not really say I was doing any good spiritually. If I left, what would these people do medically?

Where would another medical doctor come from? If I went home, I would be a failure! I had never failed before. How can I face my supporters, my church, my parents, and my family? My whole life seemed to come crashing down around me. Here I was, going to be a career missionary and I could not make it for more than thee years. How did others do it? Am I some kind of wimp? If I don't do something my family and my marriage will completely fail.

I am home! I came home and, yes, people wondered why I failed. They asked when I was going back. I couldn't say "Never!" The questions were embarrassing. People ask such personal questions. All the money my supporters gave and the prayers they offered haunted me. And I couldn't make it past one term. I am disillusioned by it all. I hope I can find a medical practice and just make it back into the normal life of a family in this country.

Sincerely,

PS: Thanks for listening. I am not writing to spread disillusionment but to let you know that missionaries are very common people. We face problems and difficulties just like any one else. And yes I find it very healing to be honest for the first time in many months.

Chapter 12

A Missionary Widow

My Dear Friend Sue,

I am alone. It is hard to believer that Charles is gone. We thought we would go together as we had served together. I look back over the years and wonder where they all went. We came out so many years ago and had such wonderful fellowship and service together. After Charles went home to be with the Lord I sat down to think about what I would do. Where would I go or should I go anyplace? Of course I had to go home after the funeral and visit family and friends and see what the Lord had for me to do. It was very hard to face so many at home. Our children are scattered and several of them offered to have me come and stay with them. But I am still relatively young and have a lot of ministry that I feel committed to.

We were called together but each of us had a definite challenge to serve the Lord overseas. We heard the Lord call and we felt we were prepared to go. We were not vocationally trained to be Dr.'s or teachers but were nevertheless called to go. We left our home country, home state, home town and home church. We left all. The zest we felt as we headed to the field will be something I will never forget. Even now I feel it in my bones as the fulfillment of a call directly from the Lord of the Harvest.

Charles also had no doubt he was to go and neither of us would look back from the plow the Lord put in our hands. It was as though the plow had two handles and we both took hold of "our" own handle with both hands. We sought to guide the plow, digging up, turning over the hard parched soil of the souls of men and women. We often looked at each other but never looked back. That in itself was a source of great satisfaction to us both. The lines were not always straight as we each felt a special calling and a special ministry. We never went different ways but we did jerk the handle a few times. We did not always do the same things as we were unique people and were gifted differently

When the children came along we had some adjustments to make that left that row not exactly even and straight. But we worked through those things and again the harmony and the cadence of our ministry came back to our gait and we plowed better than we ever had before. We would go home on furlough with the children and feel the sense of call and accomplishment thrill us again. We often spoke of what the Lord had put in our hands, how we had worked together and sensed that we had many, many years of service together ahead of us.

Charles was such a loving man with infinite patience and the ability to think like the nationals. He could sense their emotions and feelings like few other missionaries we knew. He had learned the language well and many said he spoke it like a native. I was sure that with such a capable person serving so sacrificially the Lord would leave him here for a long time to come. We occasionally talked about retiring and how out of the question it was. We both had learned a lot of lessons and were veteran missionaries with so much to give and so many lessons behind us. Surely the Lord would let us serve to old age and we would quietly pass away having "finished the work" the Lord gave us to do. Oh! How I hoped it would be that way. But "His ways are not our ways nor His thoughts our thoughts."

The Lord took him at such an important juncture in all of our lives. I still wonder how it is possible that he is gone. The children need him so much and I wonder how I can carry on without him. He had such wisdom for the children and many other young people. The children are in the midst of making some of the most important decisions of their lives. They were facing choices of vocations, mates and beginning the immense task of bringing children into this world.

Of course we often spoke of the joy of grandchildren and the wonder of having our own. Charles would have made a great "grandpa." He loved children and gave himself to the national children so often. They loved to have him around. He fixed their toys and played little games with them. What a harvest of souls the Lord would have given in all those little boys and girls if he had lived longer. I cannot help but think of the influence he would have had on any grandchildren the Lord might have given us. I never had a grandpa and we so looked forward to playing with and spending time with those our children might give us.

What amazes me is that the national people do not appear to really miss him. They seem to think that it just happens and so life carries on. They do not understand what a loss it is to the work and to the ministry. Don't they realize how important he was to their lives and the church in this area? I guess because of that they do not know my emptiness and sadness. They lose so many in their family that it does not seem to faze them or affect their thinking. They cannot seem to look into the future and realize how it might have been if Charles had lived. They carry on and do not even ask if I miss him or am lonely. I guess it is their culture. And I thought I knew their culture. I wonder what they think of me in this situation?

I know we did not seem to have time to spend with our own children as we wanted. But the mission work was so urgent and we wanted to learn the language, understand the culture and get on with the work. I guess we always thought we would have "time" in our sunset years to give our grandchildren what we did not give our children. It all looks a like a bad ending to a wonderful play. It all seemed to go so well. We were at the place where we could think of being away more and have the time we wanted with others including our family. Then all of a sudden Charles was gone.

There we were on the mission station with peace among all the folk. Some of the young men were coming on well and after a few years we would be able to turn over some of the responsibilities to them. Charles spoke often of the next term as being one of the most important ones as far as the work is concerned. What a happy ending of our lives and ministry if we could have had two or three more terms of service together. Slowly handing over the work piece by piece and encouraging them to take the responsibilities and grow into the ministries would have been ideal. We would then be able to go home for furloughs and come back for a few more years and sharpen skills, work out problems and see more of the young people established in the faith. There were a good number we wanted to see fulltime in the work and we had planned to try to support them and see them fully developed and carrying on what the Lord had given us so many years ago.

OH! I am sorry, Sue. I know I am just rambling on and wishing for what we had planned for our lives and the finishing of our ministry. I know it is selfish to even think these things but they go through my mind all the time. Everything I do I always ask myself "How would Charles have responded and how would he have handled it?" What would he have said and where would he have gone with it? What words of counsel would he have given? But it is no use going over it again and again. It cannot be and I must learn that.

But what do I do now? Can I stay here and carry on the work we began? Obviously, I can't do what God called Charles to do. I cannot disciple the young men he had such confidence in. I cannot preach and travel around the area visiting all the ones that need encouraging. What am I to do? One of our children wants me to come and live with her. We could get along well I think but it seems like I am just giving up and going home. She is single and we could work it out, I guess. What would I do? I can't start a whole new life and find something to do. I can't get a job to support myself. I would have to learn to drive all over again after driving out in the bush all these years.

Another daughter says I should live with her but it would mean living in an area of the country I just cannot stand. She is not very committed to the Lord and it would be a battle for me to want to give my time to the church and she wanting to do many things that Charles and I do not approve of for a Christian. She is dating a boy we wonder about. Our married son also asked me to consider living with them but I do not think two women are meant to be under the same roof if one is not your daughter. We do get along quite well but they have a life style of affluence and prosperity that I am very unaccustomed to as a missionary.

It is not just coming home that concerns me but leaving the mission work as well. What will happen to it if I just walk away? Charles and I have put our lives into it and to just leave seems like throwing it all away. I know the Lord is faithful. But the believers are so young, the leaders so prone to go a different way and the wolves are waiting for a chance to tear the whole thing up. We do want to leave a good name and a good ministry behind. Our plan was so fitting it seemed. But now all that is not possible. How can I turn it over to younger missionaries when no one seems prepared to come and take it all over and carry it on as we have done all these years?

On top of all of that when I was home I seemed so out of place. I was at the meetings and people greeted me kindly. They asked how I was doing? How the work was going on and many other questions about our lives together. Some were not very caring in their questions. One asked "What was I going to do now?" How do I know what I am going to do? Someone else "Which of the children was I going to live with?" Another one "You won't need as much money with your husband gone, will you!" I was floored that someone would think that let alone say it to my face. The young people do not even know who I am. They do not know what missionary work really is and don't pray for missionaries. I find it very disconcerting.

The leaders of the church just don't seem to know how to handle me or my case. They were kind to me and spoke thoughtfully but they have not offered any guidance about what I do now. I have not had a meeting with them. I am not asked to give a report of our work.

I have ladies Bible studies on the field and many are helped. But I was not asked to give a study at the ladies meetings at home. I was not asked my opinion on missions or missionary work. I was not asked about the needs of missionaries. I still have a lot to give but no one wants to know. I am reminded that "a prophet is not without honor except in his own country."

Charles always took care of the money. He handled the checking account, paid the bills, sent acknowledgments for each gift, did our taxes and paid our social security and a lot of other things that made me very dependent on him. At times we had very little money and wondered how we would make it from month to month. Other times we had an abundance and were able to help a lot of others who were serving the Lord. But I do not know. "What will my needs be?" one elder asked me when I was home. I was shocked. What does he mean? Does he think I should just come home and take the burden off the missionary offering. I have got to live even if I do come home. I am no where near the age where I can draw social security.

I cannot look after the truck, I cannot care for the computer. I do not know how to shop in town for the station. I do not know who to give money to. I cannot keep all the workmen busy on the station. I cannot move into town and just leave a lifetime of work and the station to deteriorate to nothing. Sue! please pray for me and for the work that is to be done here! I just cannot do it!

My heart is full of so much that bounces off the walls of my mind. Sometimes the thoughts never stop. I lie awake nights just thinking about it all. I could always ask Charles and he gave me a soothing answer that let me know he was in charge and it would all work out. He was so strong. But the house is empty and quiet here on the mission station. The table is empty. The bed is empty.

It seems like life is empty. I know I have Christ, but at times I need someone to hold me and talk to me and squeeze me and let me know I am loved.

Well I guess I have given you most of what is on my heart. As I said, I do not have anyone to talk to and so just had to write a note to you. I had no idea I would carry on this long. Please do not feel badly toward me for telling so much. But I have no one who will listen much less understand. Thanks for listening.

With special love to a very dear friend,

PS: But I must say sometimes I feel like it would be great to join Charles and not have to answer all these questions. Please forgive me if that is wrong.

Chapter 13

A Prepared Missionary

An open letter to our home church.

Thank you for all you have done to make our service to the Lord so effective. We look back on almost 15 years of service here on the field and find it remarkable the impact you have had on our lives. The way in which you have helped us along from the first day until now is so much like the concern and care the Thessalonians had for Paul. I feel I must write to you and let you know what a blessing it has been to us.

We are now in our early fifties and look back on a wonderful time of ministry as missionaries. I know most missionaries do not write about the way they have been led and how it has all worked out but I thought it might be helpful to others to see the pattern of our life. No! We are not done yet, but the Lord has impressed on us the need to share our thoughts. We have often been reminded of the servant of Abraham who said "As for me, being on the way, the Lord led me." We committed ourselves to the way and the Lord clearly guided all along the way.

Yes, we made many mistakes that I will not recall even though we learned a lot of special lessons from those experiences. We have failed some tests the Lord gave us and realized some important things from those personal tragedies. We were criticized for our unorthodox preparation. But surely the Lord can use for His glory what went right in our lives and service.

Jan and I met in college while we were both very keen for the Lord. I was raised in a very worldly home where God was only an occasional swear word. My parents felt like living was the goal of life and so they and our family did it to the full. Our weekends were for pleasure and we lived it to the hilt. It was late in high school when someone was interested enough in me to invite me to church and there I took Christ as my Savior. I had one year left in high school to live for God. With the help of special friends I tried to make a difference.

Jan was brought up in a Christian home that was largely the opposite from mine. Her parents were in church with her family every time the door opened. She came to believe in the Lord Jesus Christ as her Savior rather early in life and set her mind to please the Lord.

We met when we were in the cafeteria of the university. I saw Jan and some of her friends bow their heads for prayer before they ate. That impressed me and so I began "following" the girl who prayed. The Lord brought us together a few months later when she was eating alone and so was I. She had given thanks for her food and I had done the same. I asked if I could join her. She accepted my company and the rest, as they say, is history.

Jan was preparing to be a teacher and I an engineer. We graduated with the determination to give ourselves to the Lord for His service wherever it might take us. After we graduated we married and both of us began our jobs. We found an average size church where we both would be able to be involved. We were sure we would end up on the mission field but did not know when.

It was our conviction that our time in the assembly was to prepare us for missionary service overseas. Jan was pressed into service as a Sunday School teacher and I began to help with the young people.

The Lord gave us fruit from these ministries and we found our home open to the young people almost every weekend. The Lord gave us children and we found this expanded our role in the church. We were now more attuned to the young couples who were looking for fellowship where the issues of the family were addressed. We naturally flowed into a Bible study for young married couples with families. Our two children were a source of special joy. Though we both came from large families we decided that we would have a smaller family so the burden of our support would not be so much when the Lord did move us out to the mission field.

It was in a discussion of missions in this small group Bible study that the Lord laid a particular country on our hearts. We began to pray about it and found our hearts were one about this conviction. We began to explore the possibility of serving in this country and how we would best fit into its missionary needs. We had prayed about a number of countries but the Lord confirmed this area through his Word and through the affirmation of other believers.

We found ourselves looking at articles on this county in the encyclopedia and browsing the internet so we could gain a thorough knowledge of the customs, culture and needs of this country. It was encouraging as we shared our desire that many others added to our knowledge by their interest in our exercise.

By the time we knew the Lord had called us to a specific country for missionary service I was already a deacon and was plunged into many church activities that helped me know the functions of the New Testament church. With the other deacons we studied the Scriptures to see what our responsibilities were. Our home was open and we found ourselves ministering in a very practical way to many in our church and neighborhood. As a couple, we found a need for very sensitive care of widows, singles and many who were having a difficult time financially and socially.

In order to prepare for missionary work we decided to sign up for an evening class in the language of the country we were planning to serve. Though we knew we were called, we did not sense a strong urge to get to the field as soon as possible. We rather were content to make as much preparation as possible before we left our shores.

At this point we had to make many very important decisions that would shape our whole life as a family. Many around us were buying bigger houses, at least two cars, putting in a swimming pool, sending their children to expensive private schools, going into huge debt for furniture and possessions, committing to a host of extra activities and things that put roots down so deep that it would be hard to move. We were challenged in each of these areas and many others.

First we chose to stay in our simple home even though it is was crowded for the four of us. We felt the Lord had put us in this community as missionaries as much as He had called us overseas. We had been investing a lot of time and effort in friendship evangelism and did not feel it was God's plan to move to a bigger and better place just because others were doing it. We bought a big wall-size world map so we could keep the country before us and pray for the situation there. "Our Neighborhood and the World" was our motto printed on the bottom of the map.

We also chose to have Jan become a full time mother, " a homemaker," shortly after the children were born. Since I had been promoted, my income was more than adequate and because of that we could have afforded a much larger house and two cars. We chose to limit my overtime so I could invest more time in the children. Jan continued to have a lot of freedom for fellowship in the church and the community. Several of our neighbors had come to Christ and were now happily involved in our church.

Another decision we made was to send our children to public schools. Many in our fellowship were either sending their children to Christian schools or were home schooling. We were strongly condemned by these when we decided to send them to public schools. Our choice was born out of our commitment to missions and the biblical injunction to "go into all the world . . ." We were criticized for this decision but I will not go into that because this is a positive letter. We believed that we should teach our children in very practical ways what it is to be a missionary. We came to the conclusion that if the Lord called us to be missionaries then the whole family must share this burden even if the children were young. We prayed much and were convinced that it was a contradiction to be really committed to missions and not as a family be committed to that calling in our public schools long before we left for the field. "Our school and the World" was added to our motto.

Each day as the children came home from school we discussed what they learned and how the life of a believer was challenged by what they saw and were taught. They were faced with what they knew was not in their Bibles. In first grade we addressed the issues they met there. As they graduated into each class they were faced with more difficult things and bigger challenges to their faith. They showed remarkable spiritual growth. Each night after the evening meal we would have a Scripture reading and prayer. We discussed the day at school. We often prayed for their school mates. They saw their friends at school as their mission field and they entered more and more into the calling we as a family had for our mission field. They were thrilled when some of their classmates came to Christ and became a part of our church. Their maturity at church was far ahead of many of those they went to Sunday school with. How we thank God we made this choice.

With our children we continued to see how we could prepare for the eventual move overseas. Many folk who knew our call wondered why we had not gone already. Were there some problems? Did we not have enough money pledged? and a lot of other questions were asked. This did not bother us at all. We felt the Lord had slowed us down in order that we might consider long term preparation for this service.

More and more during this time I was asked to speak to the church. I found the need of a lot of time in study and preparation for ministry. Many nights I was up past bedtime because of the need to prepare a message for the next Sunday. My job also shifted somewhat as I found my latest promotion allowed me to be more flexible in my time on the job. My boss was happy to let me set my own schedule as long as I got the job done. The Lord prospered my vocation and I found time to visit the widows and others in the church who were hurting while I was traveling in my job. We were amazed how the Lord worked out so many things to promote our preparation and still meet the needs of our family.

We decided that we would have one day at home for speaking the language we were learning. We bought tapes and CD's of language study and listened to them. Our classes at the university were very helpful. We reserved every Thursday as language day. A short wave radio was tuned to that language all Thursday. We tried to make it a fun time. Our scripture reading on Thursday after supper in the language was rather slow to start with. No one could speak English to another member of our family that day. A slip of the tongue in English meant putting a quarter in the bank on the table. It was frustrating at first but the children again entered in and learned more quickly than we did. We went to a restaurant which served food from the country when we got enough money in the bank.

We chose to set aside extra money I had earned from bonuses and advancements, so we could make a trip to the country the Lord has called us. Our first visit was an amazing experience. We saw so many things and learned so much. We tried our language and were surprised how much the people appreciated the fact we were learning their language. One of the highlights was visiting missionaries we had been corresponding with over the few years. We surveyed the country and tried to find out where we would fit in and what our ministry might be. As a result of that visit we saved our vacation time and money and took several trips before we actually left for the field.

As we were able we began to support a couple of missionaries in the country. We chose missionaries that were not from our church and who had a family about the same age as ours. The children always prayed for this family. It was great to read their letters after our Bible reading and know what they were doing. Maybe we would be doing the same we often thought. A highlight was a visit from one of these families. They stayed with us. It was really crowded in our house but the children found it so much fun. We decided each morning would be reserved for "our" language. But it was nice to talk in English in the afternoon and evening.

After our second trip the elders of the church asked if I was willing to serve as an elder. Though I was a bit younger they pressed me and we discussed the implications. They reviewed my beliefs and the gift of teaching the Lord has given to me. They asked about our commitment to the church and missions and wanted to know how being a elder would fit into that calling. They felt that the Lord has given Jan and me shepherds hearts and they, in recognizing this, believed they should give the us opportunity to exercise that concern. After several months of praying about it we accepted the burden of sitting with the elders. We sensed a real peace in this decision even though we still knew we were called to overseas missionary work.

The next five years served to solidify our commitment to missions. Our children were now fully aware of how the Lord called us and they were excited about the move to the mission field. We found the church was becoming more and more in harmony with the decision we had made almost 15 years ago. We realized time with the elders allowed us to get some practical insights into the function of a church.

As an elder I was forced to work through many problems and difficulties of the church family and community. We faced many struggles of people and how the scriptures addressed them. Jan had become a skilled counselor with her own knowledge of the scriptures and the problems of life. Many came to her seeking her care and love. We realize now the Lord was building into our lives the skills of leadership that are so desperately needed on the mission filed. As an elder I had sat down with some missionaries our church supported and found many problems that we might well face as we went out. The Lord used this time to help us understand the mission field and missionaries and enter into the struggles they have in a foreign culture. This helped to sober us and let us realize that though we had been preparing for a long time we were by no means fully prepared to go. We knew we still had much to be learned on the field. But we do look back and realize that time was well spent getting ready for the job of being a missionary in a foreign culture.

One of the most important aspects of our "Preparation" was the job and working environment I experienced over those 15 years. The Lord taught us about handling money and its real value. We learned to do without some things we might have wanted. The demand to live simply, because Jan was not working, was a very good atmosphere to grow in while preparing for missions. We learned that we could save for special items instead of going out and buying on a credit card. We did not upgrade our car or our computer as soon as we might if we had two incomes. The Lord helped us in our commitments by giving me a boss who understood and promotions that were better then expected. We both agree the Lord honored our faith because we were trying to honor Him.

As an elder I did have the opportunity to talk to a number of missionaries who were struggling early in their missionary career. Many had never worked a real job for a long time and were not able to realize how much it took to live or serve. They did not seem to understand how many people in a church sacrificed in order to give to missions. The elders were amazed at the long lists of things missionaries "had to have" before they went to the field. Some, of course, never made it to the field because of the unrealistic designs of their ministry. Others think there is an endless supply of money floating through the church.

The men of the church also became a very important part of the preparation for me as the ladies did for Jan. I became accountable to them as leaders and teachers and in a position of leadership the accountability to them grew. When we were sent out that accountability only seemed natural to continue. And it did! We felt so much a part of the church that even when we were on the field we knew we were accountable to each one of the leadership and to the church as a whole.

Whenever we were home on furlough we were again welcomed back into the leadership and continued to learn as well as add the insights we had gained on the field. As a missionary I was obviously responsible for many of the activities and the leadership of the church on the field. To be home and welcomed back into the leadership, even if it was for only a year, made me feel so needed. The leadership valued my experience and I was always asking them how they handled the problems at home. We valued their wisdom in so many areas. The bond we both felt was such a profound help in our lives and ministries. When we were home we met regularly with the Bible class and met many of the new ones that had come to the church while we were gone. Our elders recommended that we spend the largest part of our furlough with them in our home church. They expected us to just melt back into the fellowship and be used where we are needed and find time to be with our family and friends. They have been such a strength and so supportive of our every need.

As for raising funds we did not have to even consider this. So often when I was an elder various missionaries came by to ask if we would support them on a regular basis if only a very small amount. When we did go out, the church rose up as one and expressed their commitment to our needs. Though they never did give me a specific figure of monthly support the church collectively gave and many individuals also added their support. They were sending out one of their own! We can look back and realize our long term preparation was one of the greatest blessings of the church being one with us in our ministry.

The elders and the church were reluctant to see us off but they knew we were called, knew we prepared as best we could, knew the church was behind us and the family was ready to go. As we sat down to figure out exactly what we were going to do on the mission field the realization came over us in a most wonderful way.

It was strange to us that what we had been doing for the past 15 years we were going to continue to do on the field. The conclusion was almost overwhelming. We were going to do exactly the same things we had been doing all this time! The same needs, the same gifts, the same goals, the same problems. Just a different country and culture. We discovered the Lord had been training us at home for service on the field. It seems so right, so practical, so Biblical. The transition was so smooth.

We have visited missionaries who have had to learn the skills of leadership in a culture that is totally foreign to them. The price is often very high in terms of casualties. No! We do not have it all right but we look back and realize the Lord honored our calling over the long term. He directed our preparation over the long haul and the ministry overseas was as normal as each and every day we spent in serving the Lord at home.

Now we look back and say with the Scripture "Hitherto hath the LORD helped us!" No we are not done. But do feel our story will be a great help to many others who want to have as practical and useful a preparation for missionary work. We did not follow the usually prescribed pattern. Finish university, go to Bible College, get a degree in missions, then raise funds and then go off the field. Ours was a very different preparation. But we thank God for every aspect of that preparation.

We are not the only ones who have been sent out by that church. The picture I have drawn for you is not the only case. Several others have seen the wisdom of long-term preparation for long-term service. The church has had the joy of sending out three other couples who have seen the need of developing their skills of leadership at home and then as leaders leaving for the field. That causes the church to accommodate the younger men and women into the church bringing them up to the level of leadership. The healthy church at home is a glorious result and qualified leaders going out is the blessing on the field. We are honored to be a part of such an effective plan for the church at home and on the field.

Others have asked us "Don't you think it was a waste of 15 years that you could have been on the field and learning the language while you were younger and sharing the gospel?." "Isn't the time short for the open door of the gospel? "Don't we have to get the job done as soon as possible?." Of all the things I could say the last would be "It was a waste." In fact I would say those fifteen yeas were the most profitable of all my Christian experience. Yes we made mistakes. But the most profound lesson of all those years and the succeeding years is that what the Lord was and is doing in my life is far more important then what he was and is doing through my life.

The Lord has now added to our family as our children have married. They finished their schooling in an international school on the mission field. Then we came home for a while to get them started in college. They have done well and found the fellowship of a church as necessary as we did when we were their age. They are very supportive of our staying on the field. They look back on their childhood and realize they had a wonderful privilege of growing up in the a healthy home, a balanced church and developed their own missionary concern in their schools.

As we look back and think about the most important things that have shaped our lives and ministry we count the strong church which allowed us the opportunity to develop our gifts and abilities as the primary institution. Our church required a strong level of accountability yet gave us many responsibilities for service. Choosing to live "below our means" and send our children to public schools gave us a "neighborhood culture" to develop our missionary commitment.

Both Jan and I have a group of men and women who grew in the Lord with us and who know our strengths and weakness and are the strongest part of our service team. We can tell them anything and they will understand and seek ways to strengthen the weakness and overcome the discouragement. They know how to pray and what to pray for us. We have the utmost confidence in them and their wisdom. We rely on them while we are on the field and when we are home.

There are a lot of other things we could share like renting our house when we left, the church sending out regular prayer letters, keeping up friendships with those who moved away from our home town. All of these and many other things have been the Lord's provision and made our lives full and satisfying.

I suppose we still have another ten to fifteen years of service to the Lord and we trust it will be the most profitable of all. If that is the case we know our church as a whole has been the prime reason we still are useful in service to the Lord on the mission field.

What can you do for missionaries? I only say that if you can in some way fulfill for other missionaries what you did for us, you will be of more use than anything else in their service both at home and on the field.

With a Biblical plan like this in place the Elders of many churches could be sending out their leaders and continue the spiritual life cycle of sending and preparing others till the world hears the gospel. We are not satisfied but like the Apostle Paul says to the Philippians we say, "I press toward the mark for the prize of the high calling of God in Christ Jesus" (Philippians 3:14).

May the Lord encourage your hearts because you have helped us prepare in a wonderful way to serve the Lord effectively. When we all get to glory your share in the reward will be great. But it will all "be found to praise, honor and glory at the revelation of Jesus Christ . . ."

We serve with joy,

PS: Doesn't it seem realistic to send out the leaders of the church today as they did in Acts 13?

Chapter 14

You Could Have Helped!

Here is how you can help!

You have had time to read and digest the forgoing "letters." Have you let yourself go enough to formulate an answer to these kinds of letters? The problems are very real and many have been "watered down" as one missionary said to me. Many of these situations have been met in a church setting and we respond with a very awkward stance and our body language tells the truth of our inability to understand, accept or handle it.

Your emotions have been involved if you have read with any insight at all. Some have shed tears; others have become very angry. Sympathy has gone out to many. Most of us have squirmed as we tried to enter into the reality of missionary minds and hearts. But these kinds of responses do not really help. Most of us have not forced a piece of paper in front of us to fill and send across the gulf that separates us from the missionary and his dilemma. We can fill the page with big words that say "WE ARE PRAYING FOR YOU!" That is suitable, acceptable, and expected but may be hollow and empty for some of us.

May I make a few suggestions for us to consider as a means of helping our missionaries as partners. Many missionaries would like someone to listen to them without making a judgment about what they are saying. The bulk of effective counseling is accepting what a person is without condemnation even if he says things that are highly charged. A missionary, like all people, need someone to listen. Our society is not learning the skills of listening. Most of us enjoy hearing ourselves more than anyone else!

A VISIT!

Our most flippant remark about "How are you?" is classic. We do not want to know! When a missionary is asked "How is it going?" We do not want to know. Yet this is the key to helping a missionary. It may not be convenient to have the missionary read a letter to you while you are standing in the church foyer. But to meet the missionary for lunch in a quiet place will give you the opportunity to listen and he to talk. It will have to be repeated for him to know you really care.

But you say, we do not have the answers. You do not have to have the answers but you have to care. Missionaries like other people want to be accepted. That is why they cannot write letters found in this book. A missionary will cautiously open a small box of problems and see how you respond. If you are not filled with fear or condemnation they will open another and another until they can fully trust you to love and accept them no matter what. This process can take a long time. But it is a much needed ministry.

A further help is what we call affirmation. All of us want to be affirmed by someone who means something to us. As children we were far more motivated by praise than by condemnation. A missionary needs to know that what he is doing is worthwhile and due praise. "You are doing a great work!" will be remembered long after "What are you doing that for?" We cannot always praise everything we hear from a missionary in a context of confidentially pouring out of their heart. But we search for something that we can affirm, a special part of their ministry or commitment that we consider worthwhile and can be commended. This is not hard to find when we think of the sacrifice most have made to go across the seas.

A missionary wants to know there is someone who really understands. Just to say we do is a trite response without foundation in most cases. As we listen we must pick up on some item that will help bridge the gap from our ignorance to their experience. Our family, our church, our service or job must have some relation to the problems the missionary is facing. What the missionary is going through is not unique to life even for a believer. To be understood a person must know that his situation is not uncommon and the Lord and others have dealt with it before.

Accountability is probably the greatest element of helping a missionary who might respond as described in this book. Accountability is not necessarily a sense of approval of all that is happening. In fact a strong part of real accountability is the freedom to make corrections and recommendations of change to someone else. This level of accountability is developed over a long time where trust is at the very heart of the relationship. As various "boxes" of problems are opened we each watch the other to see how it will be received. If affirmation is still present even if disapproval is evident, progress in the relationship is being made. A strong relationship cannot be built on nothing but approval.

When a missionary is home on furlough it is a strong case for helping if you will commit to meeting each week or each time he is in town. This is not easy but is the foundation of a relationship that can be carried on even after the missionary is back on the field. It is then possible to build on this connection through the mail or phone.

True help demands time, commitment, a listening heart, trust and honesty. To spend time with someone in itself helps them have a sense of worth. A discouraged missionary thinks they are worth little to anyone. For you to spend time with them builds a sense of worth and opens the door to real help. As they gain a sense of worth in your eyes you will build into their lives a sense of worth to God as well. Their service to the Lord and the people is a reason for worth but is often overlooked as a missionary seeks approval from you.

Confidentiality is key to real effectiveness in a ministry of encouragement. The views and feelings that are shared are a sacred trust and cannot be shared with others. We have faced the most bizarre situations and still keep a tight lip about what is going on. We have had opportunity to give a word of caution or exhortation but they are few and far between. The missionaries who ask "How do you think we are doing" are usually the ones who are doing well by our estimation. Those who are "failing" seldom ask and are often the ones who think they are doing the best work.

For some missionaries it will be a long time before they can open their heart. A man needs a man and a woman needs a woman. Ideally a couple should also have some input for a couple so the healing can be to both members of the team. Your home must be open and available to them when the need is recognized.

The last thing a missionary needs is a "sermon." They know the Bible and have preached more sermons than most of us have heard. But personal prayer with them following a thought from the Bible is quite in order. Missionaries can be slack in prayer with others as evidence of real personal communion. Praying for each other as a commitment in the midst of honest confession brings power to a relationship. Simple prayer without sincerity is just repetitious phrases which we all hear and say too well. Rather than a sermon a simple verse with a forthright prayer is a great uniter and healer.

A LETTER?

But you have a letter in front of you, not a visit. You are staring at a letter the likes of which you read in this book. True, you will more likely be able to get in a visit with a missionary where they will talk than you will receive a letter like the ones I have included. In all of my connection with missions I have never read a letter approaching the content of the ones you have read here. But I have sat down with many who spoke out of a heart filled with what is in these letters. Most of us do not get to visit a missionary and ask at his kitchen table "How is it going?" Hence this book. But should you get a letter what should you write back?

By all means write back. Not to return a letter is the greatest condemnation of the open confession you have read. A letter is necessary to offer some kind of affirmation that can be read and digested. A real and honest appreciation for them as persons and the work they are called to do and have done is in order. You may not have been interested in other letters since we do not remember much of what we read. It is discouraging to a missionary to have just sent a detailed letter to a church for a gift and then in a visit a little later have someone ask what they do, or where they serve.

Your letter must relate to something in his letter the Lord used to guide you in answering. Expressing some sense of understanding without a full blown confident comprehension of all he is going through is a source of pleasure to the missionary. The need to let the person know you care and do read (or listen in the previous case) is the foundation. Your letter must exude care and a desire to be a part of their lives and service. A financial gift will help the missionary know you do not condemn and judge him for his honesty.

Relating some experience where the Lord or someone helped you through a difficult time will add to the support you are offering just by writing. If the missionary is sensing failure for some reason he does not need to hear of someone who has never fallen or been discouraged. Honesty must be met with honesty even if the failure is in a different area. The Lord helps us through others as we wish help.

Praise for some aspect of commitment or service can also be put on paper with a suitable verse which relates to the ministry or sacrifice the missionary has made to serve the Lord. Averse the Lord used to encourage you while you were "down" can be a blessing to some missionaries.

Invite the missionary to keep up the correspondence with an offer to pray confidentially for the specific problem he is facing. If there is no response, write another short letter letting him know you care and want an update on the usefulness of your prayers for the situation.

As is the case with a personal visit, you cannot force yourself on anyone with the kind of problems these letters present without their opening the door. But it is our job to try the door and be welcomed in to exchange greetings, praise, problems, and corrections in the context of a strong relationship.

A MOTHER

Perhaps "the mother" is the person in missions who can be positively helped by a personal visit or a positive letter. Few missionaries feel as unfulfilled in a vocational way as a mother who accepted the call for missions yet is doing "motherly" work full-time.

For such a person the scripture is clear that the choice of marriage is a choice to put my spouse ahead of my ministry. 1 Corinthians 7:33 is transparent when it says "He who is married cares about the things of the world—how he may please his wife." It is hard to accept the impact of this divine declaration. So often a woman who felt called to the mission field as a single lady is mentally driven to serve with all her energy at all costs. This same mind set is carried over into marriage when Mr. Right comes along who is equally committed.

They serve together and experience a level of satisfactory fulfillment until children come along. The added responsibility of children does not always put to rest the total devotion of all a mother's energy to missionary work. The conflict of heart and mind results when the children are not seen as the primary mission field. Because the fullest load of care for children falls initially on the mother the unfulfilled burden of missionary work is also carried by the mother. A wise father will shoulder as much of the burden as possible allowing the mother to gradually realize that their primary commitment is to their children.

A host of parents have faced this battle, many times putting the ministry above the children because they have put their ministry above their marriage. If Paul teaches that a marriage places a ministry in second position on the priority list then it is reasonable that the addition of children puts the missionary endeavor further down the list. Too often the father abandons the joy of parenting to the mother since he has "the ministry" to attend to. This only relegates the mother into a darker cave of uselessness for spiritual ministry even to her children.

Obviously our personal relationship with Christ is primary above all other relationships. But the marriage relationship comes above the relationship with the lost whom I am trying to reach, or the believers whom I am trying to teach or disciple.

The conflict is often intensified because the husband/father can usually continue his work of evangelism, teaching, preaching, discipling and training the community of believers they have come to serve while the wife/mother must stop almost all community activities to minister to her children. Even as she devotes most of her time to her children her husband may feel left out. Many marriages have been seriously challenged by the addition of a child that takes the attention from the spouse, usually the husband, to the children. God has designed the mother both physically and emotionally to meet the needs of a child more adequately than a father. This division of service challenges a marriage.

The result even on the mission field is for the father to plunge more actively into missionary service in order to find the fulfillment he has lost in the family. As he immerses himself in the Lord's work the mother feels trapped in her "lowly" office of serving children. In our feminist world the dichotomy is only strengthened as women are empowered and fulfilled in a career a mother has given up, by getting married and having children.

The direction of counsel cuts right across the philosophy of the feminist to say that marriage is fulfilling in and of itself. Being a mother is a higher calling than being a missionary. If you choose marriage, and the Lord gives you children your accountability for service is shifted. When God gives children He shifts the preeminence of service from Himself to your children. 1 Corinthians 7:32-33.

It is hard in our world of self-fulfillment to subscribe to the plain statement of Scripture that the Lord accepts the transition from serving Him to serving your family when you marry and have children. A mother's [and father's] primary mission field is the children they are given by the Lord.

Many missionaries in a past generation have refused to accept this and continue to commit themselves to missionary work as though they had no children or a spouse. Missionaries have left their spouse alone while they "served the Lord" in violation of 1 Corinthians 7. Many missionaries have shipped their children off to boarding school with a view to "getting the children out of the way so they can serve the Lord." We have heard these words from the lips of missionaries. As a result some have "saved the world, but lost their children."

On the other hand there are missionaries who have continued to have children as though they had no ministry at all. Some are serving overseas as "missionaries" but have little time to do missionary work because they are investing their lives in their children. It seems reasonable for a couple with a large family to come home and raise their children instead of exhausting their resources, and the Lord's, in bringing up children on the field while purporting to be "serving the Lord." Many parents would like to "be paid" to raise their children in an exotic country far from the home-land.

Few missionaries are able to give 40 hours a week to missionary work with such a large family demanding their time and effort. For this reason parents with far smaller families see the wisdom of coming home for a number of years until their family is on their own. Then they can later recommit themselves to the work they began as a couple.

But to help the mother who is struggling with a strongly divided heart is crucial to her own well being. It is not for us to dictate to her what the family should do when the Lord holds her husband responsible. But to help a young mother see that her investment of time and energy in her children is biblical is of the greatest help. We need to help her rest in the pattern the Lord has given. Her first relationship is to the Lord as a child of God. Her second level of commitment is to her husband and the third is to her children. After these are served as best she can an added exercise could be a missionary enterprise of minimal involvement.

It seems impossible for a woman to be fully successful in so many roles even in a world where every amenity is available to "save time." To be a full time wife, full time mother and full-time career woman seems impossible even if the career is that of a missionary.

This godly mother will find her solace in the Lord and in the order the Lord has given in His word. Resting in God's direction sets her free to serve biblically. The folks back home may not understand and may wonder what she is "doing on the mission field." But her heart is settled in the ministry the Lord has given her. In the end her children shall rise up and call her blessed and her husband should praise her in the gates for her devotion to her first mission field.

We have sat with missionaries who sadly faced their family who do not know or follow the Lord because they were more concerned that the nations were in the kingdom of God then that their children were in. This pain will be carried to their grave and the sadness will no doubt be carried to the judgment seat of Christ.

Our contact with missionaries continually involves reminding them they are "doing a great work." Perhaps the greatest work results in seeing your children walk in truth because you have devoted yourselves sacrificially to them which meant much to their hearts and lives. It is a greater joy is to have your children in the family of God than to feel fulfilled by a standard set by the world, the church or even the mission board.

OUR CHILDREN

They are our most precious possession on earth. But they are developing in a culture that is so foreign to them and to you. They learn to accept our standard of living, the kind of clothes and the vastly different civilization they live in. When we are home on furlough our kids take quite a beating. They are often out of touch with the sports and fads of our home country. They must go to the meetings when we are home and they feel like they are on show. They must behave because we as parents know our lives are often judged by our children. But they feel out of it many times.

You could influence them by being interested in them and relating to them. Few people show any real interest or concern for our children. You could help us by spending time with them. By encouraging your kids to relate to our kids. You can show interest by remembering their birthday. Ask them to stay over night at your house with your family while we are home on furlough. Take them to fast food places when you take your children. Give them a subscription to a sports magazine for the boys and a suitable magazine for the girls. Let them know when you are going to a camp where they would have a good time physically and spiritually.

Choose a missionary family who have children about the same age as yours and take on the responsibility of relating to them. Try to envision their life and yours. Check on the differences and similarities. Teach your children how to pray for missionary kids. Have your children send the missionary family some money that the child can use as he wishes, sort of "fun money." Send a small parcel of things that the kids would enjoy. If you really relate then the missionary family will feel a responsibility to come and see your family when they are home on furlough.

LOVE ONE ANOTHER

We are called to minister to one another which includes to help, encourage, serve, exhort, rebuke, carry and to pray for one another. The ministry of the body of Christ should be no different to missionaries than to the members of the Body of Christ in our own local fellowship. People in every culture and spiritual station need to know they are loved and we are the means of communicating that love. A summary of 1 Corinthians 13 will outline our responsibility to each other but above all to those who have left so much of life's comforts to bring the love of God to folk we many never meet.

1 Corinthians 13

v.1 Though I speak with the tongues of men and of angels, but have not love, I have become sounding brass or a clanging cymbal.

v.2 And though I have *the gift* of prophecy, and understand all mysteries and all knowledge, and though I have all faith, so that I could remove mountains, but have not love, I am nothing.

v.3 And though I bestow all my goods to feed *the poor*, and though I give my body to be burned, but have not love, it profits me nothing.

v.4 Love suffers long and is kind; love does not envy; love does not parade itself, is not puffed up;

v.5 does not behave rudely, does not seek its own, is not provoked, thinks no evil;

v.6 does not rejoice in iniquity, but rejoices in the truth;

v.7 bears all things, believes all things, hopes all things, endures all things.

v.8 Love never fails. But whether there are prophecies, they will fail; whether there are tongues, they will cease; whether there is knowledge, it will vanish away.

v.9 For we know in part and we prophesy in part.

v.10 But when that which is perfect has come, then that which is in part will be done away.

v.11 When I was a child, I spoke as a child, I understood as a child, I thought as a child; but when I became a man, I put away childish things.

v.12 For now we see in a mirror, dimly, but then face to face. Now I know in part, but then I shall know just as I also am known.

v.13 And now abide faith, hope, love, these three; but the greatest of these is love.

Chapter 15

Pray For Us

Dear Praying Friends,

I have been deeply concerned about my personal need for your prayers. We as missionaries all ask for prayer for the "ministry," for our "service," for the "work" and many things related to what we are doing. But we do not often ask you to pray for us, at least not specifically. It just comes out of our lips "pray for us." It is much easier to say that than expose our very definite struggles and the difficulties we face as people called "Missionaries." You do not need to be told to pray! You do not need to be told when to pray! You do not need to be told where to pray! You do not need to be told why we should pray!

We do need to be helped with what to pray. The bookshelves in Christian bookstores are loaded with books on prayer. Few of these deal with what a believer should be praying.

In my travels as a missionary very occasionally I have come across a person whom I did not know till then, who says, "I pray for you every day!" Those are some of the most encouraging and humbling words I can hear.

On other occasions someone will say to me "We will be praying for you." this I also appreciate. But if I know this person well, I may ask "What do you pray?" That has created an embarrassing moment for some. They do not know what they will pray.

For us, as the Lord's servants, it is very consistent with Paul's example to ask people to pray for us. Paul asks every church to pray for him except the Galatian church. The author of Hebrews asks for prayer. Since we are told to pray many times in the New Testament it is reasonable that we would be concerned about what we pray. I have come back to the field after a furlough and attended many prayer meetings and conferences where prayer is a major concern. During the course of my year at home I decided to make a study of what people pray! When I look at my findings I am discouraged. Another missionary home on furlough said to me she went away from a missionary prayer meeting completely shattered by the content or lack of it in prayer. What is more disappointing is when I tried to convey the results of my study with Christian people the response was very abrupt and challenging even though I presented Scripture for each point. More than any other aspect of my teaching ministry while I was at home, I have experienced resistance to change and a lack of desire to learn what to pray.

The results of this study, which you can do with equal simplicity, is that the most common phrases in prayer are "Lord be with............" and "Lord bless............" Both of these are words repeated by young and old alike in most every situation and condition whether of a spiritual nature or a physical one. "Be with the Dr. .... in surgery," ". . . be with the preacher in his sermon," ". . . be with our missionary in foreign field" etc. etc. With monotonous regularity these vain expressions were repeated endlessly. We do not need a professor of theology to remind us that "He will never leave us nor forsake us." Do we need the Word of God to teach us we need not pray that He would "be with us" since He lives in us and we can never lose Him nor He us?

The second phrase of "Lord bless" is used with equal monotony. Again the scripture is plain and simple: "He has blessed us with all spiritual blessing . . ." Most mean "bless" in the sense of escaping some problem, delay, difficulty, sickness, struggle or strenuous encounter. Occasionally we use "bless" when we mean prosper, hurry, encourage, and a host of other thoughts in the same line of thinking. But to pray that we would escape a trial may be praying against the designated will of God for that missionary. The Lord has promised the path to Christ-likeness is a path of suffering, tribulation and sorrow. Besides, we sing "Draw me nearer nearer to Thy precious bleeding side" and quote "That I might know Him . . . and the fellowship of His sufferings," then pray against getting so close to His suffering side.

I was driven to the Scriptures to see why the pattern exists or what is the Biblical plan of praying. Paul makes it clear that we are "blessed" because of our faith in the God of Abraham. Galatians 3:9. A review of the blessings of the Abrahamic covenant can be seen to be fully satisfied in us though the indwelling Christ. Peter also reminded us that we have received "all things that pertain to life and godliness" Surely this is Peter's way of saying "We are blessed." To continue to ask "the Lord to bless" us, His word, the preacher, the missionary etc. is not only praying in a way that is hard to measure but praying for what the Lord has already given the believer in Christ or promised us as His children. To pray "Lord bless ...." is as unbelieving as to pray "Lord be with ...."

As I tried to share these findings with various believers I was not prepared for the response. When I faced Christians with these simple ideas from Scripture and reason, invariably it lifted some dandruff. Folks said "The Lord knows what I mean," or "The Lord wants us to come as little children in prayer" as a missionary over 70 years said to me. Or "Why does it make a difference what we say?" Or as one said to me "You want to really make prayer hard don't you." And another "This means we will have to think about what we pray!" Or as one elder said to me "I'm not going to pray in front of you anymore." Still another "Then what are we going to pray!" That last one is the question we seldom ask with a real desire to learn the exercise of praying.

On the other hand, no other subject I have taught has received so much appreciation as trying to help people pray intelligently and biblically. As missionaries we do want people to pray for us and our ministry. Many have come with special appreciation for the simplicity of these truths. Others have told me "It is right there in the Bible, why didn't I see it." One sweet new Christian said to me "That is one of the first things the Lord taught me." Another told me, "Your ministry released me from a burden I have had about saying the same things over and over again." Because of these comments and many others I am exposing my heart about my desire to have you pray for us.

If you asked most Christians if they believed in "prayer," with one voice they would say "Yes!" If you asked if they believed in "praying," a little different emotion is evident. Believing in prayer is like asking someone to pray for you. Believing in praying is doing it ourselves and gathering with a church who is doing it. We know the prayer meeting is usually the least popular, gauging by attendance. Perhaps the prayer meeting is the smallest because it is the least vital in the life of the church. It is one of the best barometers of the vital signs of a local church. That is what concerns me and many other missionaries and why I write.

What should you pray for us? What do we want people to pray for us? We are not left without guidance in this question. We have several inspired prayers of Paul that are worth studying and serve as a Biblical guide for our prayers. In fact one of the chief reasons they are preserved in the scripture is that we may follow Paul's example as we pray for fellow believers and missionaries in particular. Take a few minutes to follow my findings from the Scriptures and from my own life on what to pray for missionaries.

First, pray that they would be sensitive. One of the great tendencies of the Christian life is to become hardened by monotony. Our ritualistic repetitions are a prime example how easy it is to loose touch with reality in our prayers. This sensitivity must be directed to several areas of the believer's life.

Primary among these areas is the person and ministry of the Holy Spirit. To be insensitive to the ministry of the Holy Spirit is to "grieve" Him. His ministry to us is guidance, teaching, activating our memory, comforting, convicting, correcting and above all controlling our being through His filling. A great danger in the life of a missionary is to be insulated from the Spirit's ministry through our own ability, through repetition of a task, by pride, or because of sin which has cauterized our conscience to the Spirit's prick. The Spirit can be quenched as 1 Thessalonians 5:19 warns us. It is possible to have someone living with you and become so accustomed to their presence that you no longer confer, consult or consider their wishes or choices. This "taking for granted" is a major problem in marriage and why it is in the same context as the filling of the Holy Spirit in Ephesians 5. So it is with the Holy Spirit dwelling within us. The sweet gentle presence of the Holy Spirit can be missed so easily by busyness of missionary life and the "work of the Lord." Pray that we would be sensitive to the Spirit's ministry in our lives.

Another aspect of sensitivity is the impact the Scriptures should have on our lives. The Lord Jesus said in His prayer to the Father in John 17, "I have given them your Word." What a trust the Word of God is to the missionary and every believer. We would not be here if it were not for the Bible. But I find it can lie on the table or desk and not be consulted or read, let alone be a source of instruction and correction. Even for the preacher and missionary the Bible can seem almost a secular book used for the purpose of preparing sermons and Bible studies. The Scripture is as honey, fire, a sword, water, bread, gold and a hammer but only for those who are sensitive to its message for themselves. Familiarity with the words of the text can all too easily insulate us from its sweetness, warmth, sharpness, cleansing, filling, value or blow! Pray that we would open our eyes of understanding when the Word of God is opened whether in public preaching or private reading. We can become so familiar with the "truths" that our initial response to the Word is to judge the messenger rather then let the message judge me. Pray that we as missionaries would be sensitive to the Word of God.

A third area of sensitivity that we should address in our prayer is toward other believers. The saints are a large company of people from every walk of life in every country on earth. The ones closest to us usually give us the greatest opportunity of being insensitive. James says that faith which does not respond to the needs of the family of God is dead. John questions, if we do not attend to the distress of a brother or sister, does "the love of God dwell in us"? Paul repeats the injunctions to serve, carry, harmonize, exhort, and pray, using the familiar two word formula "one another." The interdependence the Lord wants in His church could not be better communicated than in Paul's use of the words "one another" about 44 times. This interrelationship is also strongly portrayed for us through the metaphors of the Body of Christ and the Building of God. But it is a constant temptation to be so engrossed in our own "ministry" or "service" that we become insensitive to others in the body.

The biggest problem on the mission field is missionaries getting along with each other. A host of areas of conflict and adjustment to one another come into view for intercession to the thoughtful person. There is so much hurt in almost everyone who claims to be following the Lord. Missionaries are "hurting people" if we would be honest as I am trying to do. Examining our own lives and tendencies makes for powerful prayer for others since we are "subject to like passions as others." These proclivities are exposed to our own heart not only so we can deal with them but also so we can "bear one another's burdens and so fulfill the law of Christ" in meaningful prayer. Pray that we would be sensitive to the Saints, especially those that are not too "saintly." And some of us are not always "saintly missionaries."

A fourth influence in our lives that we can be so hardened against is the sinner around us. "The whole world is lost in the darkness of sin" we sing with gusto but pass by a long list of people who lie under the Wicked one. Even those of us who have committed our lives to missionary service or "Full time Christian work" can be impervious to the calls of the lost. The call is seldom by saying "I want to be saved" but more often through loneliness, hunger, disease, rejection, and substance abuse. To be able to hear that cry and know that the gospel is the medicine that will best "lift them out of the mire into the choir" demands spiritual sensitivity. A missionary doctor in a dispensary treating 250 patients a day often loses sight of the spiritual hunger in a feverish body. A school teacher on a mission station does not always interpret the tears of a missionary's child as loneliness because she has such caring parents. A pastor that has so much to do and must screen everyone who calls or visits often forgets that he entered the ministry to care for people. Those in the "business" of saving souls are a target for callousness in dealing with the very people whom they want to "convert from the error of their way and save a soul from death and cover a multitude of sins." I meet missionaries who have had house help for years and do not seem to care if they really know the Lord. The needs of believers can keep us so busy we fumble the needs of those who do not believe. Pray missionaries would be sensitive to the cry of the lost humanity that cross our path daily.

As we pray for sensitivity in our intercession we should also pray for submission in our heart and life. The scripture informs us that true sanctification is effected by faith in the Word of God, which is translated into submission demonstrated by obedience.

An examination of most of the NT prayers demonstrate that the content of these prayers is not asking God to do some supernatural spiritual work in the life of the believer without their desire or decision. Many of our prayers suggest that God should be like a surgeon and do some spiritual operation on the believer while he sleeps under some divine power. More often the prayer of the New Testament is like asking a patient to go to the Dr. and obey, submit, learn, accept or apply some clear Biblical truth. Of course it is much easier to have the Dr. cut away the "weight . . . which so easily ensnares us" under an anesthetic rather then for us to lay aside the weight by spiritual exercise and divinely encouraged self control. The parallel to the problem of overweight is not taken out of context since the word "weight" can be understood as "fat" in the metaphor of a runner in Hebrews 12.

An example for us is Paul's prayer that the Colossians would be "filled with the knowledge of His will." Do we expect the Lord to put a funnel up to our mind and pour in His will? Obviously not. To know the will of God involves a significant dedication of time and effort to the primary source of the will of God - the Bible. It is usually the one who keeps his Bible shut that is pleading with God to reveal His will. One of our fellow missionaries said to me that knowing the will of God was the most difficult part of his Christian life. He has been serving for 28 years! I was shocked! My prayer should be, that the missionary would see the need to know the will of God and commit time and energy to learning the book and so know God and His will. The better I know my father the better I know what he wants me to do. One follows the other like the cars of a train follow the engine. For most believers it is not a supernatural revelation of His will we need, but a quiet understanding from the Word saying "this is the way walk in it." The problem is not so much God's unwillingness to reveal His will to me but my unwillingness to obey or submit to what I know already. Much or our prayer seems to infer that we are standing patiently waiting for God to say "do this" "go there," "buy this," "say that," when in fact most of us would have to admit He has already said "give this" "sacrifice that" or "deny ourselves" and we have not done it! Pray that we will do that aspect of the will of God we know.

Other scriptures support the premise that our need is to do what we know. Ephesians 1:9 reminds us that the Lord has already ". . . made known to us the mystery of His will." That is past tense and must at least refer to the Word of God as the chief source of His will. The same book tells us in 6:6 that its requirement is ". . . doing the will of God from the heart." God has already given to us at conversion all that is necessary for doing the will of God since He ". . . has given to us all things that pertain to life and godliness, through the knowledge of Him . . ." The well known Romans 12:1-2 reminds us that the sacrifice of our bodies and rejecting worldliness will "prove what is that good and acceptable and perfect will of God." Without that sacrifice can we expect the Lord to use us to be the display of His perfect will? We want His will without the painful costly sacrifice. It was when the sacrifice was laid on the alter that fire fell. The same is true for us "no sacrifice - no fire." Or as one said "God's fire only falls on a sacrifice."

It is reasonable and biblical for us to pray for each other that we would submit to the Word of God above all else. Almost every time I take up the Word of God I am faced with some general or specific requirement of submission. We have come to accept the idea it is reasonable Christian obedience to choose among the many requirements of Christian behavior rather than respond with complete obedience. As Stephen Olford said "Partial obedience is total disobedience." It is easy for me as a missionary, to become callous to the demands of the Bible and see its dictates as meaningful for others since my message is being prepared for a special congregation. Too often when I look in the mirror of the Word I see my brother! It is not how much of the Word of God I know, but how much I do that the Lord commends in John 13, "if you know these things, happy are you if you do them." Most of us missionaries could spend a very long time applying our wills to what we have already learned instead of continuing to increase our knowledge which has a tendency to puff up and harden us.

A third area that flows through prayer life is the request for strength either for missionaries or in intercession for others. In my "survey" this was right up with some others as repetitions in praying for missionaries. "Lord strengthen ...." It seems reasonable to our minds, programmed by hearing for a lifetime someone praying that the Lord would give strength to a missionary or various other believers. My mind went to Paul's prayer that the Colossians would be "strengthened with all might." Perhaps again we have been conditioned by repetition not to question our application of such a prayer. It at least causes us to be satisfied that we have helped a person in a area of great need to pray "Lord strengthen ...." or "Lord give strength to ...."

But a review of the NT promises clearly remind us, the indwelling Christ is the power or strength we need to live the

Christian life, whether as a baby in Christ, a missionary, or a fully mature believer. Do we, in fact, need extra divine strength as a special gift for unusual service? Or has God already given us the resources needed to do all He has asked us to do? Paul proclaimed he "can do all things through Christ who strengthens" him. And he reminds Timothy that God has given us the "spirit . . . of power . . ." And Peter who did not always use the available resources says "His divine power has given us all things that pertain to life and godliness . . ." We are commanded in Ephesians 6:10 to "be strong in the Lord and the power of His might," not to pray for power! The prayer for more, when He has given us all we need, seems a little forgetful, thoughtless or just plain unbelieving of the teaching of the Word.

Does this not cause us to conclude that the prayer we offer ought to be directed toward the appropriation of the resources we have already been given? Paul's injunction to the Corinthians was to be ". . . steadfast unmoveable . . ." The need to understand and apply the power we possess against temptation is one area of special need. We are prone to ask the Lord to remove the temptation or we are encouraged by some to bind the enemy so that he cannot tempt us. The need in the life of the missionary is not to remove the temptation but to avail myself of the "way of escape" which the Lord has provided. The "way of escape" is given to us whether it is the flesh whose advances we are to flee, the world's pressures we are to defeat by believing in the next world, or using the "shield of faith" to quench all Satan's desires to overthrow our faith. The Lord did not pray that Peter would not face temptation but that his faith would not fail in the temptation. We can accept that pattern for our prayers for each other. Pray for us that we would appropriate all the resources we posses to live victoriously and serve the Lord as missionaries. The temptations on the mission field are just as strong as anywhere else. Just because we are "missionaries," we don't have any more armor or any secret weapon not available to other Christians. We are tempted by the flesh to satisfy ourselves in the same way as any other person. We are just as capable of producing the "works of the flesh" on the field, as is evidenced by the moral failure of some missionaries.

The temptation of the world is just as strong in a land dotted with mud huts as with skyscrapers in an industrialized country. Self preservation has a strong pull that is very real to us as we go about the "Lord's work." Satan would like me to serve in my own strength just as he appealed to Adam and our Lord. Self-sufficiency is one of his oldest weapons, but we can be prepared for his fiery darts by presenting the "shield of faith" in the Word of God and resist him "steadfast in the faith." Pray we would "take the whole armor of God."

It is common for Christians to pray that the Lord would "bless" various people that come to mind. The word bless is used in the sense of prospering, or more often we mean the escape of any trial or problem that may come in the context of sickness, suffering, or something that would hinder the progress of the "Lord's work." To ask the Lord to remove a trial is to forget that the Lord may have sent it and promised that a person living a godly life would experience tribulation in the world and persecution from the enemies of the cross.

The need for missionaries is to make it through the trial or test God has allowed or sent for our learning and development. Pray that we would override or ride through the trials the Lord brings into our lives. The Lord could have kept the storm from coming on the sea of Galilee just when the disciples were told, by Him, to get in and go to the other side. He told them to get in and go, but He also controlled the winds and waves so they would learn to rest in the God of peace. You can pray that the missionary you are interceding for will learn the lessons of the test rather than escape. The trial is not only for our learning but also so God can point the lost as well as younger believers to a mature believer as an example of victory and maturity in the midst of problems. Pray that I will not want to escape the training and teaching He has defined for my growth.

If the primary goal of God for every believer is likeness to Christ, then the curriculum for development must be similar to the study program the Lord Himself went through at the hands of the Father by sinful man. Read Hebrews 5:8.

Simply put, we should pray that the display of the fruit of the Spirit would be manifest in each other. The fruit of the Spirit in contrast to the works of the flesh come from the garden of spiritual development. The word "works" suggest the factory of human endeavor producing the natural product of a fallen and depraved mind. In the same way that the works of the flesh are produced by the inborn raw material of self, the" fruit" of the Spirit is produced spontaneously by the inborn spiritual "materials" of the person of Christ resident in the life of every believer. We do not need more resources to produce the graces of Christ called fruit, but to cease from our own efforts and rest in the spontaneous ministry of Christ releasing His life through my life. Review Hebrews 4:10.

So again, your prayer for me is not for God to infuse further empowerment for each exercise but that I would allow the release of the strength I have in Christ and thereby the life of Christ will be "manifest in my mortal flesh." This will fulfill the purpose for which Christ called Paul in the first place, "to reveal His son in me" and complete the desire of Paul for the Galatians as well "till Christ be formed in you."

In addition to praying for us that we would overcome temptation, pray we would overwhelm the enemy. Being on the mission field seems, at times, that we have invaded the territory where the enemy has enjoyed great success. I do believe that he has as great mastery at home but with different tools of war. Because we are in "undeveloped countries," many think they are strongholds where conflict is particularly strong. In these areas we need to know that we can "quench all the fiery darts of the wicked one." The prayer we need you to pray for us is that we would be obedient and "take all the armor of God." It is there for our use, but we are tempted often to do things in our own strength because we have done it so many times. We are tempted like King

Saul giving David his oversized armor to use. Our faith is often more in ourselves than in the Lord. There the enemy can get the advantage.

Praying for missionaries is no different than praying for other believers. The goal of our prayer must be in harmony with the goal of God for that believer, Christ-likeness! If it does not lead to that, we may be praying out of harmony with the will of God and inconsistent with the Word of God. We must also consider that the Lord is wanting to teach us some very important lessons even as we serve Him as missionaries. There is no thought of being excused from tests just because we are "the Lord's servants" or because of previous tests. If we are to learn what the Lord has for us, please do not pray we will escape the test but that we will "pass" each test. So many of us as missionaries are tempted to think when a problem comes up like sickness, delay, or the breakdown of equipment, "That's strange, we are doing the Lord's work . . ." "He surely must want it done?" "Souls are perishing with Christ and here I am stuck in the red tape of bureaucracy." "I have so much to do and here I am sick in bed!" But Peter says "Think it not strange . . ." and you know the rest of 1 Peter 4:12.

More than any thing else, we all could learn what to pray for missionaries and all believers by praying as Paul prayed for the believers who were in Ephesus, Colosse, and Philippi. This is praying the Word of God and so it would be according to the will of God.

May I repeat what I said at the beginning. "Pray for us!" Pray we will be sensitive to God and His Word, His Spirit and those we are trying to serve. Pray we will be submissive to these same elements in our lives. And pray we will appropriate all the resources the Lord has given us as believers to live godly lives in the midst of a very crooked perishing, perverted, polluted and perverse world.

I hope I have not made it hard for you to pray for us. It is my prayer that we too will continue to grow in the area of prayer and be delivered from pet phrases that have been acceptable for so long.

Please pray for us in harmony with the Word of God, according to the will of God and directed by the Spirit of God. Thus you will pray with your mind and understanding.

Sincerely in our Lord Jesus Christ who is praying for us,

Your Missionary

Chapter 16

Prayer Requests

Who to Pray for? Missionaries!

Missionaries need our prayers every day. But we often do not know how to pray for them or perhaps more accurately what to pray for those who have left home and family for foreign fields. May I suggest that one of the ways you can pray for them is according to the length of service. Missionaries have different needs often determined by how long they have been serving or their present situation in life. I have indicated a dozen categories of missionaries which will help us pray intelligently. Obviously they may overlap. As you pray for a missionary think of their station in life and glance through the suggestions for that group.

CANDIDATE MISSIONARIES

Pray that as they consider going out to the field they will be sensitive to the Lord and where He would have them serve. Pray that they will believe the Lord can give them guidance not only through needs but through the Word itself. Pray they will listen to veteran missionaries in choosing a field of service. Pray they will not choose a field based strictly on emotions, convenience of lifestyle, climate, or culture. Pray they will learn to rest in the

Lord's provision for their needs now and when they arrive on the field. Pray they will accept the fact that everything which comes into the life of a believer comes by the Lord's permission or by His direction. Therefore even setbacks and delays are of the Lord's choosing and can be a source of thanksgiving. Pray they will know God is more concerned with what He is trying to do in their life than what He wants to do through their missionary effort. Pray they will realize life is a learning experience especially on the mission field. Pray they will understand that the Lord may lead them to take years to prepare for missionary work. Pray they will accept the fact that waiting to serve is not a waste of time but long term preparation. Pray that the Lord would teach them that consistent involvement in the leadership of the local church is the best training for missionary service. Pray they will respond to guidance given by elders and missionaries.

NEW MISSIONARIES

Pray that this person will have a learning and serving spirit. It is easy to think that the great sacrifice a missionary has made is not appreciated by the nationals they are serving. Pray they will know, compared to the Lord Jesus, what they have given up is not really a sacrifice. Pray they will listen far more than talk. Pray they will accept the older missionaries experiences of more weight than their youthful zeal. Pray they will learn to be self disciplined, a self starter and have a submissive spirit. Pray they will overcome pride and superiority which is a great enemy of new missionaries. Pray they will be able to distinguish what is the difference between a national's culture, the western culture they come from and the biblical culture the Lord wants to develop. Pray they will not offend in this new culture. Pray they will learn to walk with the Lord in the midst of very difficult circumstances. Pray they will learn to accept criticism and correction from others including nationals. Pray they will be dedicated in learning the language. Pray they will know their children are their first mission field. Pray they will be able to handle disappointment in themselves and particularly in other missionaries. Pray they will develop an accountability with other missionaries and the home church. Pray they will be honest in giving the Lord an eight-hour day in missionary work. Pray they will overcome the temptation to quit.

SINGLE MISSIONARIES

Pray they will accept that being single is often a great help in their service. Pray that they will not choose missionary work because they are single but because the Lord called them as a single person to serve Him. Pray they will learn proper behavior for a single in their new culture. Pray they will accept the limitations of the culture and seek to serve in that framework. Pray they will not try to change the culture if it is not contrary to the scriptures. Pray they will avoid the appearance of evil. Pray they will guard their lives and activities so they do not bring discredit to the Lord or other missionaries. Pray that their loneliness will drive them to closer communion with the Lord. Pray that they will not seek romance among the nationals which may greatly reduce their effectiveness as a missionary. Pray they will accept the wisdom to go home if they must marry and are burning in lust toward a national. Pray they accept the counsel of a veteran missionary about the difficulty and stress of cross cultural marriages. Pray that the strong temptations of a single life in a foreign culture will be overcome by a consistent walk with the Lord. Pray they will know their fellowship with the Lord is more important than their own social happiness. Pray they will learn, from the stories of other single missionaries, the effectiveness they can have in many areas of missionary work. Pray they will know the Lord has not abandoned them because they remain single. Pray they will know the satisfaction the Lord gives to those who accept the special calling to serve as a single person. Pray they will overcome the temptations of the lust of the flesh in the daily contact with the opposite sex in the service of the Lord. Pray they will fill their mind with the scriptures that can give them victory in their thought life.

SHORT TERM MISSIONARIES

Pray that as they serve in a limited atmosphere the Lord is trying to teach them lessons they could not learn elsewhere. Pray they would realize they come to serve not to be served. Pray they will learn to be obedient to the Lord and leaders. Pray they will know what it is to sacrifice for the good of others. Pray they will know the important ingredients of teamwork and cooperating for the good of a project. Pray they would realize that they are there to work for the missionary or project not to create work for them. Pray they will not see this as a time for romance and social self-gratification. The Lord may use these times to show the need for a companion in life but also that they may serve without a mate. Pray they will learn the shallowness of their own love and commitment to the Lord as they see other cultures. Pray they will learn to appreciate the abundance they have at home in comparison with those they are serving. Pray they will discover what the word sacrifice means and how they can incorporate that practice into their own lifestyle long after they are back home.

A MISSIONARY "KID"

Pray they will understand that the Lord has overseen their lives just as He has overseen the lives of their parents. Pray they will accept the fact that the overall condition of their life has been planned or allowed by God to develop in them likeness to Christ. Pray they will find a trusted friend to whom they will be accountable. Pray they will re-focus on the future rather than dwell on all that has happened in the past. Pray they "will press for the mark of the on-high calling of God in Christ Jesus." Pray they will seek the fellowship of a local church that is in touch with the struggles of life as an MK. Pray they will take all the unique opportunities they have experienced overseas to build a life shaped by the hand of the Divine Potter. Pray they will learn to appreciate the sacrifices their parents have made and why they made them. Pray they will have a love for the lost in the area of the world where they have grown up. Pray they will hear the call of God on their life and make choices that are hard rather then convenient. Pray they will find other young people who are struggling with the same issues and determine to pour their life into them. Pray their love and honor for their parents will grow deeper and result in practical ways to demonstrate it to them.

DEPUTIZING MISSIONARIES

Most missionaries come home to give reports and inform those who pray for them. Pray for these that they will not see these visits as mechanical repetitions of the activities of the last term of service. Pray they will not be discouraged by the lack of interest and opportunities of reporting their work. Pray they will give up-to-date reports and current descriptions. Pray they will be honest about their report. It is easier to only give the positive aspects of their service and unconsciously inflate numbers and times. Pray they will realize this is an opportunity to "deputize" or promote people to pray more than to ask them to give more. Pray they will learn they are not primarily trying to raise support but strengthen and challenge the Christians they are speaking to. Pray they will learn to depend on the Lord rather than men even if they are Christians. Pray they will be delivered from glorying in their work to rather glory in the Lord Jesus Christ. Pray they will spend much time in prayer and study of the Word even though they have given the same report many times before. Pray they will learn dependence on the Holy Spirit who sent them out in the first place. Pray they will acknowledge their ignorance in areas where they are not knowledgeable.

MISSIONARY MOTHERS

Being a missionary mother is one of the most taxing vocations in the world. The Lord's work is added to the job of being a mother often with several children, on top of trying to be to her husband all the Scripture demands . Pray they will accept the calling of a mother as being a higher calling than being a missionary. Pray they will understand that pouring their life into their children is more consequential than seeing the world come to Christ. Pray they will know that teaching the Bible to their children is a higher priority than teaching the Bible to the ladies in the village. Pray they will know the Lord wants all of us to be real. Pray they understand that being a "show" for people is not the calling of God but the calling of men. Pray they will know the ministry they are "giving up" to raise their children will come in a fuller and more productive way in the Lord's own time. Pray they will learn that the nationals are watching the missionary's children often more than any other part of the missionary's life. Pray they will plan the time needed for their own personal feeding on the Word in the midst of the busy schedule. Pray they will never think their children are "getting in the way" of doing the work of God. Pray they will know their children are their greatest work for God. Pray they will open up to their husband with the problems they face as mothers. Pray they will learn they are accountable to the Lord and their husband far more than to the expectations of the nationals and the folks back home. Pray that their husbands will know they are as responsible for the development of the children as they are. Pray they will let the husband lead the family as God commands. Pray they will find someone who can be a confidant on the field as well as at home. Pray you can be a confidant to some missionary and carry the confidentiality that goes with the job.

VETERAN MISSIONARIES

Pray their years of experience will not translate into pride of accomplishment or methods. Pray they will continue to learn from the people they are serving. Pray they will attempt new ways of getting the gospel to the people as the times change. Pray they will learn to get along with other missionaries. Pray they will have the courage to mend relationships with missionaries and nationals which have been offended. Pray they will realize that putting in eight hours work each day in missionary work is what is expected of them. Pray they will know that the work does not depend on their ability but their availability. Pray they will know the Lord does not expect them to spend 60-70 hours a week in "the work." Pray they will not be discouraged when leaders fall, fail them or turn against them. Pray they will understand that their family is their first mission field. Pray they will know when to turn the work over to other missionaries or to the nationals. Pray they will know when to go home and let the work survive on its own. Pray they will know when to move on to another field and let the work be directed by nationals. Pray they will know when their presence on the field is not adding to the work. Pray they will understand that "the work" doesn't have to last till the Lord comes. Pray they will realize that new missionaries will not do things the same way as they have done them for all these years. Pray they will be willing to learn from new missionaries who are coming to help them. Pray they will hand the work over as Christ did to His disciples. Pray they will be humble as they realize how much the Lord has done through them.

FURLOUGHED MISSIONARIES

Pray they will not be discouraged by the state of the church they come home to visit. Pray they will accept the Lord's victory over reverse culture shock as they reenter their home country. Pray they will not give in to the temptation to show how much better the work is on the field than at home. Pray they will not be disappointed by how uninformed the church is about their work even though they have sent letters regularly. Pray they will not be disappointed by the thoughtless prayers of "Lord bless the missionaries" and "Lord be with ...." Pray they will seek to encourage a few to pray regularly than to get the whole church mobilized for missions. Pray they will not be condescending because they have sacrificed and the church is living in abundance. Pray they will not condemn the church wholesale for the lack of commitment. Pray they will not be discouraged because there are few meetings and fewer opportunities for hospitality. Pray they will be content to sit and listen to the Word than always being the one who preaches. Pray they will know this is an opportunity to recoup some of their strength, rethink their strategy and evaluate their methods of service on the field. Pray they will be sensitive to believers who show an interest in serving with them on the field. Pray they will know how to encourage folk to come to the field and help in the work. Pray they will not complain about all the things that are different in the country since they were home last time. Pray they will know not to repeat stories and show slides that are not current and up to date. Pray they will not glamorize the mission field unfairly or present the work in an unbalanced way. Pray they will be honest and transparent about their life and service. Pray they will accept counsel and challenge from elders and others who wish to help them.

"FAILED" MISSIONARIES

Coming home because of "failure" is one of the most agonizing experiences of life. Pray they will learn to accept God's forgiveness even though men may not offer it. Pray they will not accuse others or excuse themselves but humbly accept the responsibility. Pray they will regain a close walk with the Lord which will insulate them from falling again. Pray they will be able to link up with someone who will provide accountability. Pray they will know the Lord can still use them as He did David and Peter. Pray that though they may never be able to go back they will learn to assume a role of quiet usefulness in a local church. Pray they will seek the way of escape in temptations from present circumstances. Pray they will accept people who will never forget, though the Lord has. Pray the Lord will provide employment that is satisfying and fulfilling. Pray that the family will be held together to strengthen each other and show God's forgiveness and healing to the world and the church. Pray the church will demonstrate that "love covers a multitude of sins," and welcome them home as the father welcomed the prodigal. Pray the church will learn not to talk freely about the situation but pray personally and specifically. Pray for the nationals left behind who must deal with failure in a leader. Pray they will know this experience as a warning, not a license for sin. Pray they will take their eyes off of men and look to the Lord who will not fail them.

RETURNED MISSIONARIES

Why did you come back? Pray that returned missionaries will know God's direction for coming home. Pray they will know they do not need to experience the reverse culture shock syndrome if they walk in the victory of the Lord over the world. Pray they will accept the Lord's plan even if they do not understand it. Pray they will believe the Lord is in charge, if returning is beyond their control. Pray they will trust God to work out other aspects of ministry or gainful employment at home. Pray they will realize the Lord may think their work there is done even if they do not. Pray they will not be bitter against those who may have precipitated their return, either nationals, their children, elders or fellow missionaries. Pray that others will help them accept closure of a ministry. Pray they will accept the fact that not all are called to a lifetime of missionary service. Pray they will realize that failed health is allowed by God in their lives. Pray they will know their children's education is more important than their success on the field. Pray they will believe if the Lord had wanted them on the field He would have given adequate financial support. Pray they will learn the Lord may direct their steps back after an extended time of employment or service at home. Pray they will know that coming home is not failure if the Lord has directed them. Pray they will learn through this difficult time to walk with the Lord more closely and learn God's overall plan for their life. Pray they will not blame the church for failure to support them while on the field. Pray they will not be bitter against their children for interrupting their ministry. Pray they will gain victory over disappointment and discouragement.

RETIRED MISSIONARIES

Pray for missionaries who have set down the tools of missionary work. Pray they will accept the fact that they cannot continue to do what they did in their youth. Pray they will be willing to really let go of the work. Pray they will trust God with the work just as they did when they came to the field. Pray they will not hold the reins of the work from home. Pray they will learn the joy of communion with the Lord when activity is lessened. Pray they will not feel bitter because they are not in the flow of ministry at home. Pray they will not be critical of the way the church functions when it is so different from the field or when they went out as a missionary. Pray they will accept change as being a part of life. Pray they will find a ministry and outlet for their spiritual gifts and abilities. Pray they will learn that to be set aside is not to be left alone. Pray they will give themselves to prayer for missionary works around the world. Pray they will be willing to write encouraging letters to missionaries. Pray they will judiciously support missionary works financially. Pray they will be willing to promote missions in younger people. Pray they will be committed to developing an interest in missionary service world wide. Pray they will be delivered from pride for their years of service. Pray they will continue to grow into Christ likeness as they grow older. Pray their sunset years will be as beautiful as the sunset. Pray they will with joy await the coming of the Lord.

Chapter 17

Post Script

Well you have made it to the end or is this where you are starting? In either case I hope and pray your estimate of missionaries has been greatly increased and not lowered. It is easy to conclude from these letters that all missionaries are in the condition described in these letters. Obviously we hear far more of their "good reports" which challenge us and elevate them in our eyes.

If you have had your image of missionaries injured at all please go back and read the introduction again and be reminded of the climate in which these letters are presented.

If you think all missionaries are failures then get in front of a mirror like the Word of God and see how you look if folks were to really know you and your life. Be reminded that the Bible presents great characters with their failures, defects and falls. Still the Lord used them and because we read their stories He is still using them in our lives. Missionaries are not perfect nor were the "Greats of Faith" but God is using them and we should pray for them

If these letters have caused you to pray more intelligently for those who serve the Lord as missionaries then I have accomplished what I set out to do so long ago both personally in my life and ministry and these epistles. Thank you for reading them.